90573A

Data Processing
With
Applications

Data Processing With Applications

ROBERT J. CONDON
Westchester Community College

Reston Publishing Company, Inc.
A Prentice-Hall Company
Reston, Virginia

Library of Congress Cataloging in Publication Data

Condon, Robert J
  Data Processing with applications.
  Includes index.
    1. Business—Data processing. I. Title.
HF5548.2.C617   658 '.05 '4   77-10654
ISBN 0-87909-181-9

© 1978 by RESTON PUBLISHING COMPANY, INC.
A Prentice-Hall Company
Reston, Virginia 22090

10 9 8 7 6 5 4 3 2 1

Printed in the United States of America

To the Condon kids
Mary, Bob, Jim, Anne, Peter, and Tom

Contents

Preface

Virtually every college business major today will encounter the computer during some phase of his or her business career. This book is designed to prepare the marketing, accounting, management, business administration, and data processing major for that encounter.

The text can be used for any introductory course in data processing. It does not emphasize the bits and bytes of computer technology, although that material is covered; rather it stresses how various business organizations use the computer to increase profit and provide better services.

The book is organized into four sections:

    I.   What the Computer Does
   II.   Processing Data
  III.   Programming
  IV.   Computer Applications

The book is easy to read because nontechnical language is used wherever possible and technical jargon is carefully explained. The business student, regardless of his or her area of expertise, will see how the computer can be used as a tool for producing faster, more accurate, and more meaningful results.

May I express my appreciation to the staff at Reston Publishing for their advice and encouragement. May I also extend my appreciation to T. Marll McDonald of Dean Junior College and Kobad Arjani and Joseph Masterjoseph of Westchester Community College for their valued criticism. Finally, may I express my thanks to my wife, Mae, for the patience she displayed as this book was put together.

ROBERT J. CONDON

Data Processing
With
Applications

I
What
the
Computer
Does

1

The
Computer

Objectives

This chapter explains in basic terms what the computer is, how it developed, and how it is used today. From it the reader should begin to appreciate the computer's potential and limitations.

WHAT ARE COMPUTERS?

"The computer cancelled the biology class I wanted." "Let's feed it to the computer and see what it has to say." "Did we get that computer run of overdue accounts from the data center yet?" "I wish that the computer could get my telephone bill correct just once!"

Expressions similar to these indicate the extent to which the computer affects our lives. The computer is an important factor in many aspects of life today and will become increasingly important in the future.

Computers are electronic devices that perform computations and logical operations. They provide man with a powerful tool that enables him to increase his effectiveness in science, mathematics, medicine, engineering, business, and many other fields.

Business uses the computer to process data electronically. The computer is electronic; it uses the flow of electricity to represent and process data. The main advantage of electronic processing is speed. If electricity can go around the world seven times in one second, it can do vast amounts of calculations moving back and forth within cabinets no bigger than an ordinary desk.

Data is composed of facts, which, when processed electronically, provide the information required to run a business.

This book concerns itself primarily with the use of computers in business, although the machines were originally created to perform scientific calculations. The computer is the tool through which many businesses perform routine accounting, control inventories, and provide an organization's staff and its management with the information necessary to carry on the business profitably.

WHAT CAN COMPUTERS DO?

Although the computer is often described as an electronic brain, it can perform only very elementary tasks. Essentially, a computer can:

1. Perform arithmetic.
2. Store a set of instructions called a *program*.
3. Answer a question "yes" or "no," provided that the information necessary to make that decision is available to it.

Performing Arithmetic

Computers perform the four basic arithmetic functions: adding, subtracting, multiplying, and dividing. The computer is unique because

it does them at a rate of tens of thousands of calculations per second
and with almost perfect accuracy. Select the finest, most accurate
mathematician at any college and pit him against a computer in a race
to do 10,000 calculations. The computer will finish in a matter of
seconds; the mathematician will take hours, perhaps days. More importantly, the computer will almost certainly have every calculation
correct; the mathematician, through human fault and fatigue, will
make errors in doing so many calculations. The mathematician and
humans in general are not inferior to computers. A computer always
requires human assistance in the form of a computer program before
it can attempt any task.

Memorizing Programs

On its own a computer can do nothing! It is merely a blank memory
with the potential to store instructions, but with no ability to create
them. A computer works by first storing a set of instructions, called a
program, and then executing these instructions. Thus, before a computer performs even the simplest task, it must receive detailed instructions from a programmer.

For some idea of the precision required of a programmer in preparing instructions for a computer, picture a caveman being brought into
the present. The caveman may be reasonably intelligent, but he lived
in a different environment and is not familiar with today's technology
and terminology. Suppose that the caveman were brought to a car in
a parking lot and you were told to explain to him how to start the car.
How would you do it?

It is not very easy. The instruction, "Put the key in the ignition"
does not work. Imagine the caveman's reaction to that! He has no
idea of what a key is and certainly no concept of an ignition. These
terms must be explained to him. Even before this instruction is at-
tempted, the caveman must be told how to get into a car. "Open the
door" is not good enough with someone who has never opened a
door before.

The job of a computer programmer is to describe to a blank memory, which has nowhere near the creative ability of a caveman, the
detailed steps required to carry out a particular function. To do this,
every detail must be perfectly explained, and terms with which the
computer is not familiar must be clearly defined. Before he gives any
instructions to the computer, the programmer must have a perfect
knowledge of the problem and its logical solution.

Describing the computer as merely a blank memory, which can

initiate nothing, does not explain the computer's potential. The computer's memory is flexible; it can store one set of instructions, carry them out, and then store a completely different set of instructions. It can do this indefinitely. The component that stores programmed instructions is called *main memory* or *internal storage*. Main memory is part of the essential component of a computer system, the central processor.

Answering Logical Questions

Computers have the ability to examine information and answer questions about it. For example, consider a college that maintains a punched card for each person enrolled. Suppose also that the card contains a code indicating whether the student is male or female. The computer can examine each card and by checking the code determine whether the card represents a male or female. To do this, the computer requires a program instructing it precisely how to analyze each card, and each bit of information contained on that card.

THE PROGRAM AND DATA

A program to carry out the operation referred to above and to write the word "male" or "female" next to each name would look something like this:

Read a card from the file of student cards.

If the card contains a male code, print the student's name and the word "male."

If the card contains a female code, print the student's name and the word "female."

Read the next card and continue processing as instructed above until the entire file has been processed. Then stop.

Data for this task must be contained in machine-readable form, such as on punched cards or magnetized tapes or disks.

The card, of course, would contain other items of information about each student, his name, date of birth, or year of graduation, for instance, and any of this data may be analyzed and appropriate action taken. If each record contains the student's year of birth, a program could ask: Is year of birth equal to 56? Is year of birth less than 43? Is year of birth missing from this record? (See Fig. 1-1.)

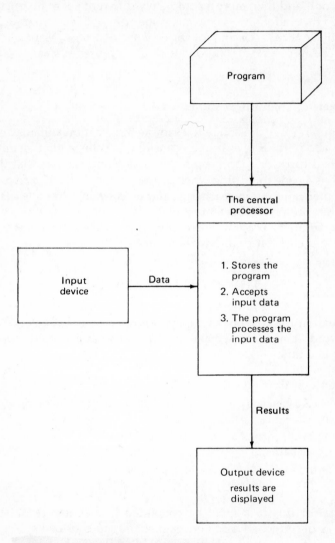

Figure 1-1. A typical computer job.

COMPUTER SYSTEMS

A computer, or, more accurately, a computer system, consists of a central processor and input and output devices. The components are connected by cables usually hidden under a false floor. Input devices such as card readers, magnetic tape units, disk units, optical character readers, and typewriter terminals bring information to the central processor. Some output devices such as printers and cathode ray tubes (television displays) record results of computer processing in a format that people can read; other output devices, magnetic tape units, disk units, and card punches for instance, record results in a format that can be read again by machine. (See Figs. 1-2 and 1-3.)

Courtesy of Hewlett-Packard

Figure 1-2.   A modern computer system consists of a central processor (center) and various input/output devices.

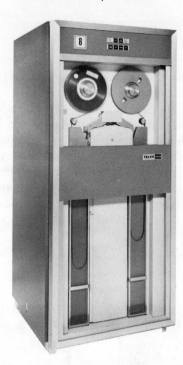

Courtesy of Telex Corporation

Figure 1-3. A magnetic tape unit that can read data from magnetic tape or write data on it.

The central processor performs four general functions:

1. It stores programs in its main memory or internal storage.
2. It does arithmetic in an arithmetic unit.
3. It performs logical functions, such as answering questions "yes" or "no" in a logical unit.
4. It also controls the accuracy of these functions through its transistorized control unit.

A typical computer job consists of four steps:

1. The central processor stores a program. The program may be contained on punched cards, magnetic tape, or disk.
2. Data is read from an input device into the central processor.
3. The central processor performs the programmed instructions upon the data, usually processing one record at a time.
4. The results of processing are displayed on one or more output devices. (See Fig. 1-4.)

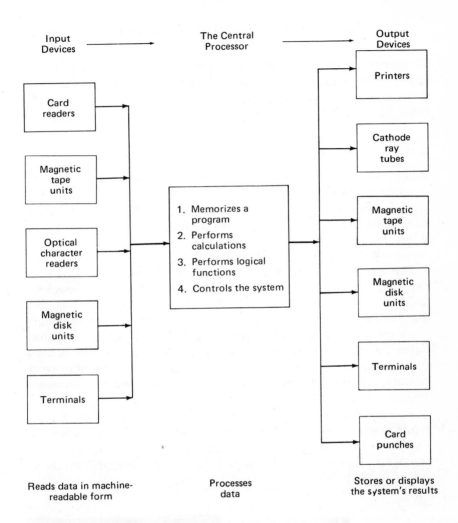

Figure 1-4. A computer system.

A computer, even a small one, is far more complex than the hand-held calculators so popular today. Computers are versatile and can process an infinite array of programs; calculators are limited to pre-wired functions. Computers accept data in a variety of forms; calculators use only hand-keyed data. Computers perform without human intervention when programmed; calculators require human input for each step.

THE DEVELOPMENT OF THE COMPUTER

The computer evolved from four independent, but related, developments: performing calculations by machine, storing data in machine-readable form, storing programs internally within a machine, and the need for rapid data processing.

Calculating By Machine

People have always searched for ways to calculate more quickly and accurately. The first calculating devices, man's fingers, were not fast enough for his needs. Early civilizations in both Asia and Greece developed the abacus, a device for adding using beads strung on wires. Although the abacus is over 2500 years old, it is still used by merchants in some parts of the world today.

Throughout the medieval and modern eras, mathematicians have experimented with various devices that perform calculations mechanically. In the seventeenth century, Blaise Pascal, a French philosopher and mathematician, developed a hand calculator that added quantities cranked into it. In the years that followed, many calculating devices were developed, but most were not accurate enough, or were too complex, for common use. In the early part of the nineteenth century, Charles Babbage, an Englishman, designed the Analytical Engine, which accepted data from punched cards, compared numbers, made logical decisions, and computed large numbers. But the world was not ready for this machine, and the design never became reality. By the end of the nineteenth century, however, it could be safely said that man had developed the ability to compute mechanically. (See Fig. 1-5.)

Figure 1-5.   The abacus.

Storing Data in Machine-readable Form

In the 1880s, a significant event took place in the United States. The federal government takes a population census every 10 years. The census of 1880 took almost eight years to complete. Estimates for completing the census of 1890 ran as high as 12 to 15 years. Starting the census of 1900 before the census of 1890 was tabulated was distinctly possible. To alleviate this situation, Dr. Herman Hollerith of the Census Bureau conceived the idea of recording census data in holes punched in a piece of cardboard. This was significant because, for the first time, data was recorded in machine-readable form. Hollerith recorded the information for the 1890 census on punched cards and processed it with sorting and counting machines he designed. So effective was this breakthrough that the census of 1890 was completed in less than three years.

Hollerith's idea of using a card to record data was not original. As early as 1801, in France, Joseph Jacquard had used punched cards to control a loom weaving threads. It has also been said that Hollerith's invention was inspired by the player piano, which produced music from holes in a roll of paper.

Bolstered by the successful conclusion of the census of 1890, Hollerith founded the Tabulating Machine Company, which produced punched card equipment for private industry and government agencies. In 1924, through a series of mergers, this company became known as International Business Machines, or IBM. (See Fig. 1-6.)

Hollerith's equipment was used again for the census of 1900, but by 1910, James Powers had developed more advanced punched card equipment for the Census Bureau. His innovation was to store an entire record in the punching mechanism until it was complete and correct, and then to punch the data into a card. This first buffer, or temporary storage device, increased accuracy and reduced the time for error correction.

Like Hollerith, Powers founded a company to produce punched card equipment commercially. In 1927, his company became part of the Remington Rand Corporation.

Punched card equipment remained relatively unchanged until nearly 1950. The equipment became more versatile, processing was speeded up, calculators—which could multiply and divide—and tabulators—which could add, subtract, and print results—were introduced, but the equipment of the 1940s was not radically different from that of Hollerith's day. The two rival companies, IBM and Remington Rand, competed head to head; IBM with the 80-column Hollerith card with rectangular holes and Remington Rand with a

Calculating by Machine	Processing Data in Machine-Readable Form	Storing Instructions
450 B.C. ancient civilizations develop the abacus		
1647 Pascal produces a mechanical adding machine		
		1801 Jacquard's loom
1823 Babbage designs the Analytical Engine		
		1850 the player piano
	1887 Hollerith's punched card	
	1910 Powers modernizes punched card equipment	
	1924 IBM formed	
	1927 Remington Rand formed	
1944 Aiken develops Mark I at Harvard		
1946 Mauchley and Eckert develop ENIAC at Penn		1947 Von Neumann's internally stored program

Figure 1-6. Development of the computer.

14

90-column card featuring round holes. IBM generally held the upper hand.

The first computers, Mark I and ENIAC, were developed independently of each other during the Second World War. Mark I, developed at Harvard University under the direction of Howard Aiken, was sponsored by IBM and the United States Navy. It was a mechanical calculator that used electromagnetic relays for controlling internal operations. It could perform approximately three calculations per second.

ENIAC (Electronic Numerical Integrator And Calculator) was the product of the Moore School of Engineering of the University of Pennsylvania. ENIAC was developed for the Bureau of Ordnance of the United States Army in 1946 under the direction of two men, Dr. John Mauchley and J. Presper Eckert. This computer was electronic, using vacuum tubes for computing. ENIAC became the prototype of all modern computers and is probably the source of the stereotype notion of the giant mechanical brain seen in many cartoons. It was enormous, occupying over 1500 square feet and having nearly 20,000 vacuum tubes. It could do 1000 calculations per second. By the mid-1940s, man had developed an electronic machine that could perform calculations. (See Fig. 1-7.)

Courtesy of the Sperry Rand Corporation

Figure 1-7. ENIAC, the first electronic computer.

Storing Instructions Internally

Instructions for processing data with Mark I were punched onto paper tape and read into the electrical and mechanical components of the computer. ENIAC's programmed instructions were wired into a board that was inserted into the machine. A major refinement, generally attributed to John von Neumann, was to store programmed instructions in a memory unit inside the computer. Thus, programs written on external storage media, such as punched cards, could be entered into the computer's memory. When the computer was finished with a program, a different program could be put into the computer's memory from other cards and a different job done.

The Need For Rapid Data Processing

In the mid 1940s, business was in the process of converting from a war footing to a peacetime economy. Business was also on the threshold of its greatest period of expansion. Industries like insurance and banking were experiencing unprecedented growth. Government agencies became larger and more complex. As business became larger, its paperwork problems expanded. The ten years following World War II are often called "the paperwork explosion." Business naturally looked for assistance to the recently created tool of science, the computer. If the computer performed calculations for the scientist and the engineer, why could it not effectively do business's record keeping? (See Fig. 1-8.)

The need for a commercially oriented computer was first answered by Remington Rand when it developed UNIVAC I. This first commercial computer was installed at the Census Bureau in 1951. By 1954, however, IBM was marketing the IBM 650, which became the standard computer of that era. During this period other manufacturers—RCA, Philco, General Electric, Burroughs, Honeywell, and National Cash Register, for instance—entered the computer field with various computer models for science and business. These computers, all of which used vacuum tubes, are characterized as the first generation of computers.

In 1959, IBM produced a computer, the IBM 1401, that used transistors instead of vacuum tubes. Transistors are much smaller than vacuum tubes, so computers using them could do more and occupy less space. Transistors required less power, did not overheat, and were considerably faster than vacuum tubes. Computers became

Courtesy of the Sperry Rand Corporation

Figure 1-8. UNIVAC I, the first commercial computer.

smaller and more efficient. Other manufacturers, particularly Honeywell with its 200 series and UNIVAC, produced successful second-generation, or transistorized computers.

IBM proclaimed the third generation of computers with the announcement of the IBM/360 in 1964. Third generation computers are characterized by a further miniaturization of circuitry that permits the computer to do more complex operations in relatively the same space. They perform multiprogramming, that is, they handle more than one program at a time. Manufacturers produced an entire range of models and designed equipment so that a customer could easily move up to a larger model as his electronic data processing needs increased. RCA answered the challenge of IBM with Spectra 70, while Remington Rand's answer was the UNIVAC 9000 Series. Soon other manufacturers came out with their own computer families. (See Fig. 1-9.)

In the early 1970s, a series of computers that were refinements and improvements of third generation equipment were marketed. These computers, which many consider the fourth generation, featured further miniaturization of components and increased computer potential. This era is also marked by the proliferation of minicomputers whose circuitry can fit on a desk top. (See Figs. 1-10, 1-11, and 1-12.)

First Generation
IBM 650

Second Generation
IBM 1401

Third Generation
UNIVAC 1100

Figure 1-9.   Three generations of computers.

1951   UNIVAC I, developed by Remington Rand, installed at Census Bureau.

1953   IBM markets the IBM 650.

1954   General Electric installs a UNIVAC I.

1959   IBM markets a transistorized computer, the IBM 1401, which ushers in the second generation of computers.

1964   IBM announces a third generation family of computers, the IBM System/360.

1965   Digital Equipment Corporation markets PDP-8, a commercially successful minicomputer.

1970   IBM/370 modernizes the concepts of the 360.

1972   Minicomputers are produced by more than 50 manufacturers.

1974   Microcomputers, whose circuitry can be held in one's hand, become commercially feasible.

Figure 1-10.   Computer developments in the business field.

Courtesy of IBM

Figure 1-11.   The circuitry of a modern computer shown with sugar crystals on a spoon. Each unit can contain 48,000 elements of information.

Courtesy of Hewlett-Packard Company

Figure 1-12.   Miniaturization of components has led to compact computer systems such as the Hewlett-Packard 3000 Model 5.

COMPUTER POTENTIAL

Man is beginning to realize the computer's full potential. It is widely used in business, primarily for record keeping. Data is gathered, processed, stored, and results are produced. For example, a men's clothing store may record sales and receipt of cash on punched cards. Each month this data is collected, sorted, and processed by computer to determine each customer's balance. A report of new balances and a billing statement result.

Business first used the computer for fundamental accounting. Companies found that computer systems maintained inventory and accounted for receivables better than the numerous clerks needed to do these tasks manually. Once the primary accounting applications were computerized, the data these systems provided were summarized and reported to management in concise form. For example, a payroll system normally provides paychecks and stores salary information for quarterly and annual tax reports. However, the system can also provide summarized information for analyzing personnel turnover or evaluating the company's recruiting program. This use of the computer is often called a management information system (MIS). (See Figs. 1-13, 1-14, and 1-15.)

Figure 1-13. A mini-computer used for cost analysis.

Courtesy of IBM

Figure 1-14. Using a computer for chemical research.

Courtesy of IBM

Courtesy of Tektronics, Inc.

Figure 1-15.   A graphic computer display used in a classroom.

The computer of the late 1970s offers untapped potential. A distributor of electrical parts can maintain accurate inventory data with a computer, but he can also produce reports analyzing vendor performance, stock turnover, and profitability by product. Consider these other types of "inventory":

- An airline maintains a count of the seats available for each flight. As each ticket is sold, the count is instantly updated, and this information is made available throughout the entire organization.
- A bank maintains the balances of each customer's account. When a teller requests a customer's balance before cashing a check, this data is provided immediately.
- A life insurance company maintains records on all of its policyholders over the past 20 years and analyzes their life span to determine equitable premium rates for new customers.

Other computer uses include:

- A school system develops a series of computer programs to reinforce learning arithmetic.

- A hospital installs a computer to monitor the vital signs of seriously ill patients.
- A manufacturer of electronic components installs a computer to measure characteristics of the parts it is producing.
- The marketing department of a major food company develops a program to analyze the effectiveness of the advertising campaign for its new breakfast cereal.

These are just a few of the many applications in which computers are used today. It seems as if the computer can do almost anything. However, it has its limitations.

COMPUTER LIMITATIONS

Specialized Use

When processing data, the computer is most effective in handling high-volume, highly repetitive work. Payroll is a typical application, since it is performed in the same way each pay period. However, if there are fewer than 50 employees on the payroll, the job would probably be better done manually. Moreover, an analysis of the turnover among the employees of a company with 500 employees might be very helpful to a personnel department, but if it is done only once and the raw data is not in machine-readable form, the analysis is done better with pencil, paper, and a desk calculator.

Cost

Processing data by computer is costly. Data must be available in machine-readable form, and data processing equipment is expensive. More importantly, qualified personnel must be employed to operate and program the equipment and insure the accuracy of its results. However, cost per transaction is usually less in a well-managed computer system than in a well-managed manual system.

Effective Management

Using computers requires skill throughout the entire organization. Not only are computer technicians needed; a company requires effective management to organize and control the computer and effectively to utilize the information that it provides.

Only a Tool of Man

The computer cannot create; it can only follow the instructions the programmer provides and can use only the data that is available to it.

Requires Extensive Systems Design

Smooth-running computer systems do not just happen. They are the product of skillful design and extensive testing.

THE IMPORTANCE OF THE COMPUTER

The computer has become an important part of life today and an essential for survival for many businesses. It has tremendous untapped potential and serious limitations. It is not a panacea for man's ills, but merely a tool that gives man the potential to extend his mental abilities.

MAKING IT PRACTICAL

Ted Barnes has been in the hardware business in Richtown Heights for over 20 years. Richtown Heights, a suburb of Houston, has grown tremendously during the past few years, and so has Mr. Barnes' business. In addition to hardware, Mr. Barnes now has a large garden and lawn center and a Do It Yourself outlet that features tools and materials.

Inventory maintenance has become difficult for Mr. Barnes. With over 6000 items in stock, Barnes has had difficulty in ordering parts and maintaining an adequate inventory to satisfy customer needs.

Last week, a salesman from a computer firm called Mr. Barnes to point out the benefits of maintaining inventory by computer. He spoke of other businesses similar to Mr. Barnes' that had successfully mechanized inventory and suggested that Barnes seriously consider installing a computer.

Mr. Barnes heard that you were studying about computers and called you for advice. He knows nothing at all about computers or how they could be used in his business. He would like you to explain to him:

1. How computers work.
2. Where they are used in business today.
3. What they are capable of doing.
4. What their limitations are.

Mr. Barnes wants only some general ideas about computers for now. What advice do you have for him?

REVIEW QUESTIONS

1. Explain the importance of Herman Hollerith in the development of data processing.
2. What four factors led to the development of the computer?
3. What were the contributions of these men to the computer's development: Charles Babbage, Howard Aiken, John Mauchley, and John von Neumann?
4. What are the four basic functions of the central processor?
5. Explain what is meant by the term "computer generation." What characteristics marked each generation of computers?
6. Comment on the expression, "Computers are smarter than humans."
7. Distinguish between programs and data.
8. List five key steps in the development of the computer.
9. List five applications in which computers are used today.
10. Explain three limitations of the computer.

GLOSSARY

Abacus—a device developed during ancient times, which used beads strung on wires for counting

Buffer—a temporary storage device

Cathode Ray Tube—a television display used with computers

Central Processor—the mainframe of a computer, which stores programs, performs arithmetic and logical functions, and controls the entire system

Computer—an electronic device that performs computations and logical operations

Computer System—a central processor and its input and output devices

Data—bits of information

ENIAC—the first electronic computer

External Storage Media—devices that store data outside the central processor

File—a group of related records

Input Devices—equipment that provides data for the central processor

Internal Storage—a portion of the central processor that stores programs and receives data from input devices

Main Memory—the component of the central processor that stores programmed instructions

Mark I—an early computer that used electromechanical relays for calculating

Multiprogramming—performing more than one program at a time

Output Devices—equipment that receives the results of a computer's operations

Program—a set of instructions for the computer to carry out

Programmer—a person who writes detailed instructions for a computer

Record—a group of related data elements

UNIVAC I—the first commercial computer

2

Hardware and Software

Objectives

Hardware is equipment—devices that make up a computer system. Software is programs—instruction sets that assist equipment in performing tasks. This chapter describes some hardware systems currently in use and demonstrates how software interacts with hardware for efficient computer utilization.

HARDWARE SYSTEMS

Computer manufacturers produce an incredible range of computer systems and an even wider range of input and output devices to satisfy almost any customer's needs. Computer systems consist of hardware, which is computer equipment, and software, which includes the specific applications programs to do an installation's jobs. Of course, *people* are the ultimate controllers of hardware and software.

Computer hardware systems are often categorized by central processor size. The term K, from the Greek *kilo*, meaning 1000, is used to describe internal storage capacity of a central processor. A "K" is approximately 1000 positions of storage (electronic "mailboxes"), each of which usually contains one character. A position of storage is often referred to as a *byte*.

People speak of medium-sized computers; of small and large ones; as well as of minis and supers. These terms are convenient, but not precise. The guidelines below are approximations for classifying computers.

Classification	Purchase Price	Storage Capacity
Micro	less than $15,000	1K to 32K
Mini	$15,000 to $60,000	4K to 64K
Small	$60,000 to $150,000	8K to 96K
Medium	$150,000 to $1,000,000	64K to 512K
Large	$1,000,000 to $5,000,000	256K to 1000K
Super	$5,000,000 to $10,000,000	1000K to 8000K

Until the 1970s, the terms small, medium, and large were sufficient for classifying computers, but the proliferation of equipment and the impact of miniaturization of circuitry demand newer classifications.

MICROCOMPUTERS

Microcomputers are a recent development in computer hardware. Microcomputers are generally defined as computers with circuitry that can be held in one's hand. Today, over fifty companies produce microcomputers for use in data communications, automation in industry, and limited business data processing. Microcomputers are used in business for controlling input/output devices such as electronic cash registers and typewriter terminals that transmit data over telephone lines, and for assembly line and machine tool production control in industry. Microcomputers are often programmed to do one specific task, such as controlling traffic lights or monitoring the engine of an automobile. This process of "dedicating" a computer to one task uses a feature called "read only memory" (ROM), which stores instructions permanently in nonerasable memory. Experts claim that there will be 15 million microcomputers in use by 1985. One primary market for microcomputers is home use, where household chores, bookkeeping, educational and recreational applications, and even electronic mail service from computer to computer are possible.

MINICOMPUTERS

The impact of minicomputers was first felt when Digital Equipment Corporation introduced the PDP-8 computer in the mid-1960s. Since then, business and industry have applied this tool to so many uses that now approximately 60 percent of all computers installed are minicomputers. Minicomputers are characterized by their comparatively small memories, slow input/output devices, and a limited number of instructions available for programming. Minicomputers are often used in business to control terminals for transmitting data to a central computer and for controlling industrial processes such as typesetting. They too are often programmed to do one specific task. More than fifty companies produce minicomputers, and it is estimated that there will be over 2 million minicomputers in use by 1985. The key to the growth of minicomputers is the development of compatible input/output devices comparable in price to the main processor. Besides the PDP-8, and its successor the PDP-11, other computers in this category include the Burroughs 700 series, Hewlett-Packard's 2000 and 3000 series, Varian 620, Raytheon 700, Microdata's Micro 800, Texas Instrument 900, and Data General's Nova and Eclipse series. (See Fig. 2-1.)

SMALL COMPUTERS

The most widely used small computer today is IBM System/3. Originally introduced in 1969 as a punched-card system for small users, System/3 has expanded its input/output capabilities to include magnetic tape and disk. System/3 uses a 96-column card instead of the

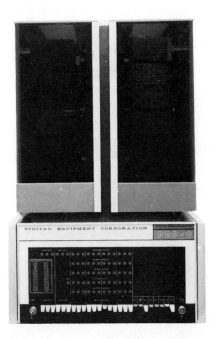

Courtesy of Digital Equipment Corporation

Figure 2-1. The PDP-8 minicomputer.

conventional 80 columns and has internal storage capacity of up to 96,000 positions of storage. Other computers in this classification include Burroughs' B1700 and NCR's Century 50. (See Figs. 2-2 and 2-3.)

MEDIUM AND LARGE COMPUTERS

As in other categories, the distinction between small and medium, and medium and large computers is hazy. The prototype medium-sized computers were the smaller models of IBM 360—Models 30 and 40. Today's typical medium-sized computers are the smaller models of System/370—Models 125, 135, and 145, for example. Larger models in the 370 family, such as Model 155, are usually considered large computers. In one respect, computer models are similar to automobiles in classification. Chevrolet, Buick, Pontiac, Oldsmobile,

Courtesy of NCR Corporation

Figure 2-2. NCR Century 50/MOD I, which is designed for first-time small-company users.

Courtesy of Burroughs Corporation

Figure 2-3. Burroughs B 1700 computer system.

and Cadillac are cars in the General Motors family. They are different products with different price ranges designed to handle the various needs of the driving public. IBM has its equivalent of the Chevrolet Chevette and Vega in its Model 5100 and System 32. Its Novas, Impalas, and Monzas are the System/3 family of computers. The IBM 370 line represents its Buicks, Pontiacs, Oldsmobiles, and Cadillacs. (See Fig. 2-4.)

SUPERCOMPUTERS

Several manufacturers market supercomputers with internal capacity measured in the millions of storage positions and purchase price near 10 million dollars. IBM System/370 Model 195, Burroughs' B7700, and Control Data's Cyber 70 series are in this class.

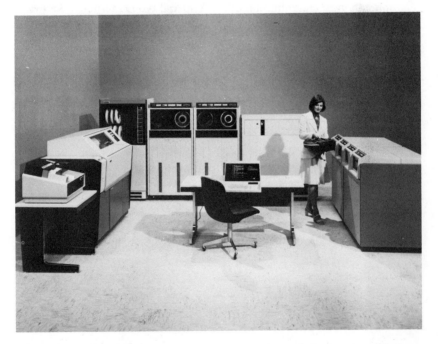

Courtesy of NCR Corporation

Figure 2-4.   An NCR Criterion 8570 data processing system consisting of (from left to right) a card reader-punch, printer, magnetic tape units, central processor, and disk units. A console with CRT display is in the center of the system.

INPUT HARDWARE

It has been emphasized that the computer is really a computer system with a central processor controlling a network of input and output devices. Some typical input devices are:

- Card readers—read up to 1400 cards per minute, but are slow compared with other input devices.
- Magnetic tape units—read data from magnetic tapes at high speeds.
- Disk units—read data from magnetic disks.
- Scanners—read printed matter. Scanners include optical character readers (OCR), which read data with photoelectric cells, and magnetic ink character readers (MICR), which read characters made from specially treated ink.
- Terminals—transmit data from remote locations over telephone lines. These include typewriter terminals, electronic cash registers, touch-tone phones, and minicomputers. A special type of terminal, known as a *console*, is used for operator communication with the computer system.

OUTPUT HARDWARE

Typical output hardware includes:

- Printers—display the computer's results on paper at high speed.
- Cathode ray tubes (CRT)—television-like displays.
- Typewriter terminals—print the computer's results at low speeds.
- Card punch units—punch computer output in machine-readable form.
- Magnetic tape units—receive output as well as provide input.
- Disk units—also input/output (I/O) devices. (See Figs. 2-5 and 2-6.)

SOFTWARE

The term *software* has many definitions. Here it is used to describe the programs used to assist computer hardware. Software programs are produced by computer users, computer manufacturers, and vendors who write them for specific needs. Vendor-written programs are often called "software packages."

Courtesy of IBM

Figure 2-5. **A typewriter terminal. The operator is typing invoices and creating computer input simultaneously.**

Courtesy of IBM

Figure 2-6. **IBM 1403 printer, which has been the standard high-speed printer since the early 1960s.**

USER PROGRAMS

Every task performed by a computer requires a program. Listing the contents of a file, solving complex mathematical problems, or printing an organization's payroll checks all require programs. These programs, referred to as *applications programs,* are written by the system's users. Over a period of time an organization builds up a library of hundreds, or even thousands, of applications programs.

MANUFACTURER SUPPLIED PROGRAMS

When a computer system is rented or purchased, the hardware configuration is supported by a set of programs. These include:

1. An operating system.
2. Translator programs.
3. Utility programs.
4. Emulator programs.

Operating Systems

Modern computers are expensive and complex. Experience with earlier models has taught that programmed routines can carry out much of the computer's day-to-day work more efficiently and accurately than a computer operator can. Programmed routines load programs into main memory, keep track of which programs and data files are where, and provide uninterrupted computer operations. Routines found in every program, such as handling reading and writing instructions, are written once and executed by the computer instead of having them incorporated into each program. Computers come equipped with a series of programs, called an *operating system* (OS), to handle everyday computer tasks.

An operating system is located on a disk unit directly available to, or on-line with, the central processor. As a day's operations begin, the operator depresses a series of keys on his console to call a supervisor, or executive, program from the disk unit into main storage. The executive program acts as a traffic controller for the entire system. It directs all programs coming into and going out from the central processor, calls for special programs when required, notifies the operator through the console when the computer system is encountering difficulties, and performs routine chores.

Today's computers process several programs simultaneously. It is not unusual for a computer to handle as many as fifteen programs and control perhaps one hundred input/output devices at one time. This process, known as *multiprogramming,* is controlled by the operating system. The operating system is programmed to allocate the central processor's storage in the most efficient way and to direct the traffic of programs and data messages to and from their allocated places in main memory.

The operating system is designed to keep the computer system as busy as possible. To do this, instructions concerning what jobs are to be done, the programs to do them, and the data files that they will use must be available to the central processor. The operating system's programs will execute the highest-priority jobs, matching up required software and hardware to use the facilities most efficiently, and then will handle the transition to the jobs that are waiting to be done. When problems are incurred, the operating system is programmed to notify the computer operator of the situation and await instructions as to what action to take.

Besides the supervisor program, an operating system includes these programs:

IPL	Initial Program Load	—the program that puts the supervisor program into main memory
JCL	Job Control Language	—converts the computer operator's instructions to a format that the computer can use
IOCS	Input/Output Control Systems	—handles routine input and output instructions
Various library routines		—store and locate programs on a disk unit

Translator Programs

Each computer has its own language, called *machine* or *actual language,* and can only process instructions in that language. The language of a UNIVAC machine is different from the language of an IBM machine. An IBM System/3 has a different machine language from an IBM System/370. Programmers have found it too cumbersome and confusing to write instructions in machine language that consists of numbers and not words, so many programming languages have been developed to make program writing easier. Translator programs, known as *compilers,* convert instructions from the programmer's language to machine language.

More than one hundred programming languages exist today, because programmers' needs are so varied. Some well-known languages and their uses are:

COBOL	COmmon Business Oriented Language	uses English language terms for processing business applications
FORTRAN	FORmula TRANslation	solves mathematical problems
BASIC	Beginners All-purpose Symbolic Instruction Code	a simple language for remote terminal use
RPG	Report Program Generator	prepares basic business reports
PL/1	Programming Language One	an all-purpose language for both scientists and businessmen
BAL	Basic Assembler Language	resembles machine language; difficult to learn, but uses the computer efficiently
APT	Automatic Programmed Tool	controls machine processing

When a computer is rented or purchased, the buyer knows his language needs and acquires only the compilers that he requires to translate his programs into the computer's machine language.

Utility Programs

Computer manufacturers also provide a series of programs for doing tasks that regularly occur at an installation. These include routines for sorting data, merging files, transferring data from punched cards to magnetic tape or disk, copying files, and displaying records.

Emulator Programs

An emulator program allows a computer to imitate a different computer. When a new computer is introduced and it is an improvement on a previous model, it must be capable of running the programs written for the earlier model because of the user's investment in programs for the older computer. Emulator programs give computers this capability.

VENDOR-SUPPLIED SOFTWARE PACKAGES

Because many organizations have common programming needs—all companies have payrolls, most have sales on account, and all must pay their creditors—various business organizations, including computer manufacturers, have written general programs for rental or purchase. These programming packages reduce the time that it takes a company to write its own programs. However, programming packages often must be modified, because so many companies insist on custom-made systems.

TYPICAL COMPUTER SYSTEMS

Computer systems vary from portable microcomputers to massive systems that occupy an entire floor of an office building. The systems described here, which include both hardware and software, are typical of what is currently available from computer manufacturers.

Burroughs B7700

The Burroughs B7700 series of computers are typically very large-scale or supercomputers. Designed for use in organizations with massive files and heavy data communications requirements, this computer system has become popular in processing government files and coordinating transactions in multibranch banks. (See Fig. 2-7.)

The largest model in the B7700 family, the B7780, has four central processors with a total main memory of over six million bytes. In addition, the system uses two input/output processors for controlling hardware devices. Each I/O processor can control four disk subsystems, each with a potential capacity of 5600 million bytes, up to twenty other I/O devices, and over one thousand data communication telephone lines. When working at full capacity, the I/O processors can transfer up to 6.75 million bytes per second to or from the central processor. This is equivalent to about 80,000 ordinary punched cards per second.

Courtesy of Burroughs Corporation

Figure 2-7.   A Burroughs B7700 large-scale computer.

It requires an experienced, sophisticated organization to use so powerful a tool near its full potential. A B7700 computer system is used by the Australian government to coordinate personnel administration and organizational control for public service departments throughout the country. Another system processes data for a communications network among 1100 branches of a Belgian bank.

IBM System/370 Model 145

The most widely used medium-to-large-scale computers today are IBM's System/370 family of computers. Model 145, a medium-sized processor in the 370 series, was first introduced in September, 1970. A typical Model 145 configuration consists of a main memory of over one-half million bytes controlling a network of I/O devices. Up to sixteen disk units can be connected to its CPU with a capacity of over 1.6 billion bytes of data. A typical system supports 50 to 100 remote terminals used for inquiring record status from a disk unit, or for updating records. The system can be purchased for under $2,000,000. (See Fig. 2-8.)

Courtesy of IBM

Figure 2-8. IBM System/370 Model 145.

IBM System/3 Model 10

IBM System/3 includes a group of computers for the small or first-time user of electronic computers. System/3 Model 10 originally appeared in 1969 as a punched-card machine featuring an innovative 96-column card instead of the standard 80. The system has since expanded to include magnetic tape and disk storage facilities, as well as the ability to control a small network of remotely located terminals.

System/3 is usually programmed in RPG II, a language created especially for it, but since 1971, the system can handle both COBOL and FORTRAN.

A typical System/3 Model 10 configuration consists of a central processor of 48,000 bytes, a card processing unit that can read, punch, sequence, and print on punched cards, a 600-line-per-minute printer, and disk storage capable of holding over 40 million bytes of data. Purchase price for this system is approximately $100,000 to $200,000. (See Fig. 2-9.)

Courtesy of IBM

Figure 2-9. IBM System/3 Model 10.

Raytheon RDS–500

Raytheon's RDS-500 is typical of the minicomputers currently popular. A typical configuration includes a 32K central processor with models of 64K available. Compatible input/output devices include a 1000-card-per-minute card reader, cathode ray tubes, magnetic tape units, and small disk units. The system's software permits limited multiprogramming. User programs are written in FORTRAN and SYM III, a language similar to Basic Assembler Language.

The RDS-500 is widely used in the petroleum industry to analyze data collected in search for oil. RDS-500s are also seen in production automation and process control in industry. (See Fig. 2-10.)

Courtesy of Raytheon Data Systems

Figure 2-10. Raytheon's RDS-500 minicomputer shown with two tape units and a printer.

MAKING IT PRACTICAL

You have been working in the business office of Paradise Valley Junior College as a bookkeeper for the past two months. The college has no computer equipment and maintains all its records manually.

Yesterday, Jerry Doherty, the college's business officer, told you that the administration is considering acquiring a minicomputer to maintain the school's financial records. Since no one at the school is familiar with computers and you have shown an interest in the area, Mr. Doherty has asked you to do some preliminary research on the project. Mr. Doherty wants:

1. The names of five companies that market minicomputers so that he may contact them and have a salesman call to explain the product.
2. A two-page, double-spaced typewritten report explaining what minicomputers are, where they are currently used, and how one might be used at Paradise Valley Junior College.

Mr. Doherty mentioned that *Datamation, Computerworld, Data Management,* and *Data Processing Digest* are among the trade publications available at most libraries. He suggested that you start with one of them in gathering information for the project.

Prepare the list and report requested by Mr. Doherty.

REVIEW QUESTIONS

1. What is the difference between software and hardware?
2. Explain what is meant by a *computer system.*
3. List three characteristics of minicomputers.
4. What are microcomputers?
5. What unique I/O medium is associated with IBM System/3?
6. Name four commonly used input devices.
7. What are user programs?
8. What types of programs are supplied by computer manufacturers?
9. Name four hardware devices for displaying computer output.
10. What functions do operating systems perform?
11. Why are translator programs needed?

12. What functions do the executive, or supervisor, program perform?

13. What do emulator programs do?

14. Why are there so many different programming languages?

15. What are software packages? Where are they used? Name one disadvantage associated with them.

GLOSSARY

APT—Automatic Programmed Tool; a computer language for controlling machine processing

BAL—Basic Assembler Language; a programming language similar to machine language

BASIC—Beginners All-purpose Symbolic Instruction Code; a language frequently used with terminals

Byte—a storage position that normally contains one character

COBOL—Common Business Oriented Language; a programming language frequently used in business

Compiler—a program for translating instructions from the programmer's language to machine language

Console—a terminal used by a computer operator for communication with the computer system

CRT—cathode ray tube; a television display

Emulator Program—a program that allows a computer to imitate another computer

Executive Program—a supervisor program; one that controls the traffic within a computer system

FORTRAN—FORmula TRANslation; a programming language used for solving mathematical problems

Hardware—computer-related equipment

I/O—input/output

IOCS—Input/Output Control Systems; a program for handling routine input and output instructions

IPL—Initial Program Load; that program that puts the supervisor program into main memory

JCL—Job Control Language; a program that converts operator instructions to machine language format

K—approximately 1000 positions of storage; actually 1024 storage positions

MICR—Magnetic Ink Character Recognition; a device for reading data from magnetically treated ink

Microcomputer—a computer whose circuitry is so small that it can be held in one's hand

OCR—Optical Character Recognition; a device that reads data through photoelectric cells

On-line—the status of being in direct contact with the CPU

OS—operating system

PL-1—Programming Language One; an all-purpose language for scientist and businessman

ROM—Read Only Memory; instructions stored permanently in nonerasable memory

Scanner—an input device for reading printed matter

Software—all the programs used to assist computer equipment

Supervisor Program—an executive program; one that controls the traffic within the computer system

Terminal—a hardware device for transmitting and receiving data from remote locations

Utility Program—a program that performs the routine work of a computer installation, such as sorting data, merging files, and transferring information

3

Basic
Storage Media

Objectives

This chapter explains the media used to store data outside the central processor. The reader will learn how data is represented in machine-readable form and will become more aware of the advantages and disadvantages of each of the basic storage devices.

STORAGE MEDIA

Externally stored data, that is, data stored outside the computer's central processor, falls into two categories; data that must be processed sequentially and data that may be accessed directly.

Sequential processing means that the first 595 records must be read through before record 596 is located. Direct access processing implies that record 596 can be located immediately and its data made available to the central processor. For example, a person could locate Yvonne Zullo's telephone number by starting at page 1 and sequentially comparing each person's name in the directory to Zullo, Yvonne, or he could go directly to the names beginning with ZU and then begin the sequential search. (See Fig. 3-1.)

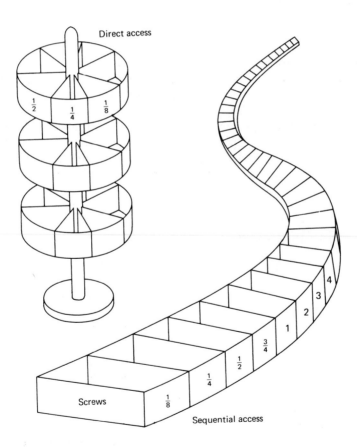

Figure 3-1. Sequential versus direct processing.

Media for sequential processing include:

- punched cards
- magnetic tape
- punched paper tape

Direct access media include:

- magnetic disks
- magnetic drums
- film strip memory

SEQUENTIAL PROCESSING STORAGE MEDIA

Punched Cards

The standard punched card was developed nearly 100 years ago by Herman Hollerith. It consists of 80 columns, each of which can contain one number, one letter, or one special character, such as a punctuation mark (Fig. 3-2). A card column contains 12 positions, or rows. The positions 0 through 9 are used for recording numbers, with each digit requiring one column. The number 765 would require three columns. To record a digit, the position corresponding to that digit is punched with a rectangular hole (Fig. 3-3). A social security number

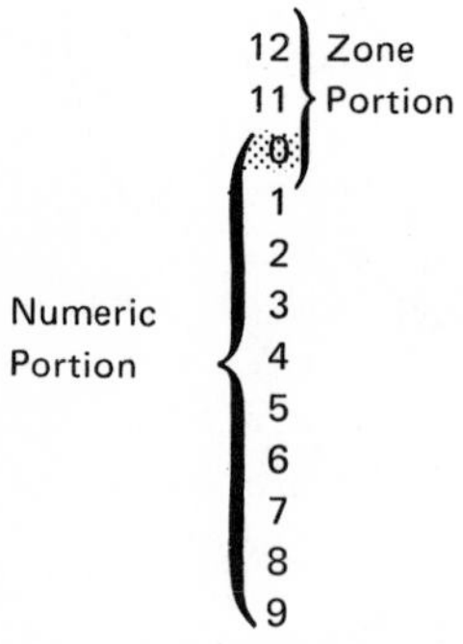

Figure 3-2.   A card column.

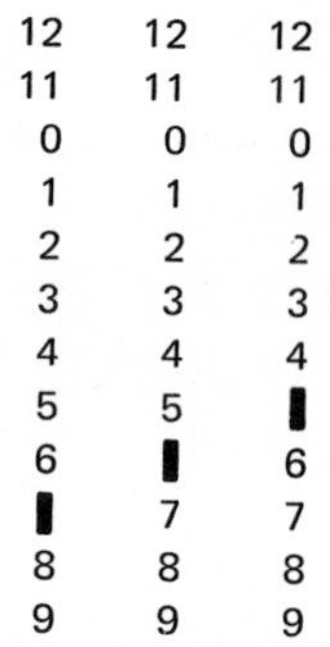

Figure 3.3.   Three columns containing the number 765.

requires nine columns. All social security numbers have nine digits, and editing, such as the dashes in the social security number, is not normally recorded in punched cards. Date of birth requires six columns: two for day, two for the number of the month, and two for the last two digits of the year.

Recording a letter in a column requires two punches, a zone punch and a numeric. The top three positions of a column are zone positions 12, 11, and 0. Note that 0 is used as both a zone and numeric position. A comparatively simple system, known as the Hollerith code, is used for encoding characters in punched cards.

The Hollerith code is as follows:

Zone Punch	Numeric Punch	Characters
12	1 through 9	A through I
11	1 through 9	J through R
0	2 through 9	S through Z
no zone	0 through 9	0 through 9

Note that numbers have no zone punches and that the last third of the alphabet (S through Z) begins with the digit 2 and not 1. This is due to a machine restriction that existed when the code was developed, namely that the 0–1 combination had punches too close together in a column.

The word SAM encoded in Hollerith code in card columns 45 through 47 is

```
    S    A    M
    12   ▮    12
    11   11   ▮
    ▮    0    0
    1    ▮    1
    ▮    2    2
    3    3    3
    4    4    ▮
    5    5    5
    6    6    6
    7    7    7
    8    8    8
    9    9    9
    45   46   47
```

The 80 columns of a punched card are divided into data fields of varying lengths. A typical student data card might contain these fields (Fig. 3-4):

Columns	Data Field	Type of Field
1–9	Social security number	Numeric
10–25	Name	Alphabetic
26–31	Date of birth	Numeric
32–45	Street address	Alphanumeric
46–55	City	Alphabetic
56–57	State (abbreviated)	Alphabetic
58–62	Zip code	Numeric
63	Veteran status	Alphabetic
64–65	Year of graduation	Numeric
66	Sex code	Numeric
67–68	Major code	Numeric

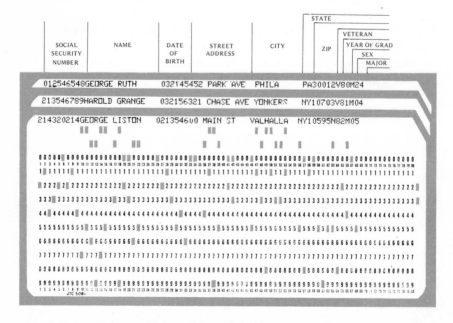

Figure 3-4. Three cards from a typical student data file.

Examine each field in Fig. 3-4. Numeric fields—the social security number, for instance—have only one punch in each column, but alphabetic fields, like the street address, have two. Notice also that there are no spaces between fields. The programmer will define field lengths to the computer before the cards are processed, so spaces are unnecessary on the punched cards.

The card also shows how codes are used. Veteran status is coded "V," which uses one column instead of the seven to spell out "veteran." Sex code is 1 or 2, or perhaps M or F. A student's major uses a two-digit code instead of spelling out the field of study.

The expression, "The computer is making a number of all of us," contains an element of truth. It requires twice the number of punches to record alphabetic information that it does to record numeric information in punched cards, although the same amount of key strokes are necessary. Recording data in numerical codes is also more efficient than spelling out what the codes represent.

IBM System/3 introduced a smaller, 96-column punched card. The 96 columns are made up of three tiers of 32 columns each. The holes in the card are smaller and closer together, and the Binary Coded Decimal (BCD) code, which uses only 6 rows, replaces the Hollerith code, which uses 12 rows for expressing each character. (See Fig. 3-5.)

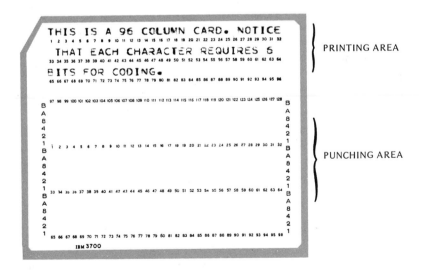

Figure 3-5. A 96-column card is coded with the 6-bit BCD code. Characters are punched in three tiers at the bottom of the card and printed at the top.

The six positions, or bits, of the BCD code are zones B and A at the top and the numerical values of 8, 4, 2, and 1 at the bottom. By using combinations of these numbers any digit from one to nine can be formed: 4 and 2 are 6; 4, 2, and 1 are 7; 8 and 1 are 9. The values 8, 4, 2, and 1 are from the binary numbering system, which will be explained later. (See Fig. 3-6.)

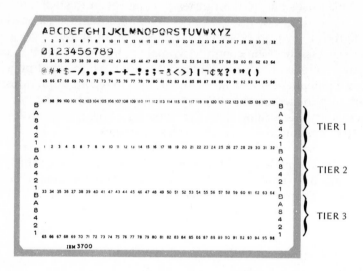

Figure 3-6. A 96-column card showing the alphabet in tier 1, numerical punching in tier 2, and special characters in tier 3.

The three zones of the Hollerith code are reduced to two in BCD:

Hollerith	BCD
12 zone	A and B bits
11 zone	B bit
0 zone	A bit

The number 0 in Hollerith is an A bit in BCD. Compare the two fields coded in Hollerith and BCD in Fig. 3-7.

The expression, "The punched card is obsolete," heard so often, is partially true. Except in very small installations, punched cards are too slow and inconvenient to use as a storage medium for a company's files. They are used today primarily for storing programs and

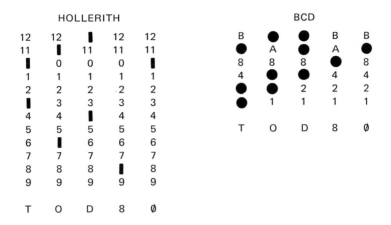

Figure 3-7. The characters TOD8∅ in Hollerith and BCD codes.

seldom-used input data. For generations business has keypunched input data into punched cards. Even though more sophisticated methods of recording data exist, such as through terminals, the punched card survives as an economic means of recording business events, especially for companies with small data processing budgets. Cards can also be read by people, since the key punch usually prints the character on top of a card column.

Magnetic Tape

Business data is often recorded on magnetic tape. Tape for recording data is similar to that used for home tape recorders. Once recorded, the contents of the tape can be replayed as often as desired. When the tape's contents are no longer needed, new data is recorded over the existing data.

Magnetic tape has two distinct advantages over punched cards as a storage medium. It holds information more efficiently; a reel of tape 10 inches in diameter and 2400 feet long can hold as much data as a half million punched cards. Data on magnetic tape can be processed more quickly; it can be read several hundred times faster than data on punched cards. Magnetic tape files have one great disadvantage; they must be processed sequentially. Consider the following characteristics of magnetic tape files.

Tape Density

Tape density refers to the number of characters, or bytes, that can fit
into one inch of tape. Standard density currently is 1600 bytes per
inch (BPI), but tape in densities of 800, 3200 and 6250 BPI exist. When
density is 1600 BPI, one inch of tape holds the contents of 20 punched
cards.

Data is coded on magnetic tape in magnetized spots either in the
six-bit BCD code or the eight-bit Extended Binary Coded Decimal
Interchange Code (EBCDIC). BCD uses seven rows, called *tracks*, on
magnetic tape, while EBCDIC uses nine. The additional track is used
by the computer for verifying data accuracy.

The eight-bit EBCDIC code provides magnetic tape with the potential to pack numeric data, that is, to put two digits within one byte.
The eight-bit byte consists of two groups of binary positions 8, 4, 2, 1,
each of which can contain a number (Fig. 3-8). This does not literally
double the storage capacity of magnetic tape when numbers are used,
because each number packed in storage must have a sign, which
requires one-half byte. For example, five-digit numbers require three
bytes to store, as do four-digit numbers (Figs. 3-9 and 3-10.).

EBCDIC coding is also used on nine-track tape to represent alphabetic characters and unpacked numbers. The top four binary digits, or
bits, are used for the zone portion of the letter, and the bottom represents the decimal portion (See Fig. 3-11.). The coding for this zoned
decimal format is

EBCDIC Coding—Zoned Decimal Format

12 in the zone	+	1 through 9	= A through I
13 in the zone	+	1 through 9	= J through R
14 in the zone	+	2 through 9	= S through Z
15 in the zone	+	0 through 9	= 0 through 9

Numerical data on magnetic tape may be either packed (packed
decimal format) or unpacked (zoned decimal format). Alphabetic
and special characters may not be packed. Packing data not only
allows for more efficient use of external storage media, but also permits data to be stored more efficiently within the central processor.
However, all packed data requires a positive or negative sign that
occupies four bits, or one-half byte, and is positioned at the right-
hand side of the numeral.

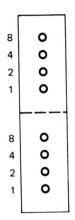

Figure 3-8. The 8-bit byte.

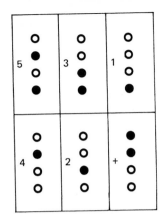

Figure 3-9. The number + 54321 as it would appear in packed form.

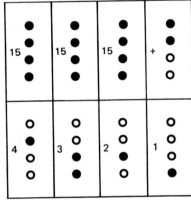

Figure 3-10. The number + 4321 in unpacked and packed format.

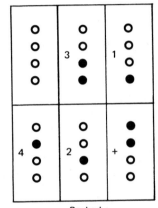

Figure 3-11. The word "SAM" in EBCDIC code.

	HOLLERITH CODE	BCD CODE	EXTENDED BCD CODE
Letters A through I	12 Zone + 1 through 9 punches	A B Bits + 1 through 9 combinations	12 Zone + 1 through 9 combinations
Letters J through R	11 Zone + 1 through 9 punches	B Bit + 1 through 9 combinations	13 Zone + 1 through 9 combinations
Letters S through Z	0 Zone + 2 through 9 punches	A Bit + 2 through 9 combinations	14 Zone + 2 through 9 combinations
Numbers 1 through 9	Blank zone + 1 through 9 punches	No bit + 1 through 9 combinations	15 Zone + 1 through 9 combinations

Figure 3-12. A summary of computer coding structures.

Reel Lengths

The standard length of a reel of tape is 2400 feet, but other lengths are common. Installations often use minireels of 300, 400, and 500 feet.

Record Lengths

Unlike punched cards, whose records are limited to 80 columns, magnetic tape records may be any length. Tape records of 200, 450, or as much as 800 characters are not unusual. Record lengths within a file may also vary. A student who has completed 30 courses at a college would normally have a longer master record than one who has completed only two.

Interrecord Gaps

The apparent advantage of magnetic tape as a storage medium is limited, because a record must be physically separated from other records by a gap. When a tape record is read or written upon, the tape unit requires about ¾ inch to start and stop. In determining the capacity of a reel of tape, the following factors must be considered:

- tape density—number of characters that will fit on one inch of tape
- reel length—number of feet in a reel of tape
- record length—number of bytes in each record
- interrecord gap length—amount of space required for starting and stopping a tape unit

Consider this tape problem: How many records will fit on a reel of magnetic tape with the following specifications?

tape density	1600 bytes per inch
reel length	2400 feet
record length	400 bytes
interrecord gap length	¾ inch

A portion of this tape would look as shown in Fig. 3-13.

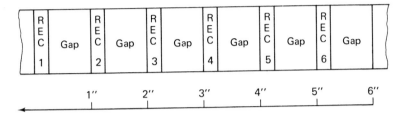

Figure 3-13. A portion of a reel of tape containing unblocked records.

Remember that each record contains 400 bytes and that each inch of tape has a capacity of 1600 bytes. Thus each inch of tape contains one record of ¼ inch and an interrecord gap of ¾ inch. If each inch contains one record, then

$$
\begin{array}{rcl}
1 \text{ inch} & = & 1 \text{ record} \\
\times 12 \text{ inches} & & \times 12 \\
\hline
1 \text{ foot} & & 12 \text{ records} \\
\times 2400 \quad \text{feet/reel} & & \times 2400 \\
\hline
2400 \quad \text{feet} & & 28{,}800 \text{ records}
\end{array}
$$

Blocking

A tape file in which most of the tape contains gaps instead of data is highly inefficient. Therefore, records are grouped into blocks, and several records are placed between gaps.

Consider this problem:

tape density	1600 bytes
reel length	2400 feet
record length	400 bytes
interrecord gap length	¾ inch
blocking factor	3 (3 records are contained between each gap)

A portion of the tape is shown in Fig. 3-14. It shows that three inches of tape now contain six records and two gaps. Now at least the tape contains half data and half gaps. Thus

$$
\begin{array}{rcl}
\text{3 inches} & = & \text{6 records} \\
\underline{\times\ 4} & & \underline{\times\ 4} \\
\text{1 foot} & = & \text{24 records} \\
\underline{\times\ 2400\ \text{feet}} & & \underline{\times\ 2400\ \text{feet}} \\
\text{2400 feet} & & \text{57,600 records}
\end{array}
$$

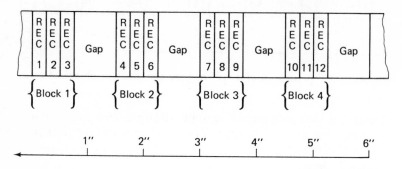

Figure 3-14.   A portion of a reel of tape containing blocked records.

By changing the blocking factor from 1 to 3, the capacity of the tape doubled.

The limitation on block length is the availability of internal storage in the central processor and the size of the programs with which the file will be used. If a computer has 16,000 bytes available for a program and uses 12,000 for instructions, 4000 bytes remain for input/output handling. If a program both reads and writes tape files, the maxiumum block length for input or output would be 2000 bytes.

In many modern computer systems, software programs determine the most efficient blocks for handling data.

PUNCHED PAPER TAPE

Punched paper tape is another sequentially processed storage medium. Data is recorded in circular holes punched into a continuous strip of paper tape. Coding is similar to BCD. Originally designed for transmitting and receiving telegraph messages, punched paper tape has had limited application in modern data processing. It is used frequently as a by-product of another process, such as recording cash register transactions in machine-readable form. Paper tape is also used to control machine processing, such as a punch press or paper mill operations, in much the same way that the roll of paper in a player piano controls the notes played. (See Fig. 3-15.)

Courtesy of Teletype Corporation

Figure 3-15. Data being recorded on punched paper tape.

Compared with punched cards, paper tape has several advantages: records are not limited to 80 characters, paper tape is cheap, it can be mailed or easily transported, and it can be read or written upon faster than punched cards. However, paper tape is a slower processor than most storage media, it can tear and break, it requires special reading and punching equipment, and it usually must be done over when error correction is necessary.

DIRECT ACCESS STORAGE MEDIA

The most prominent storage media used today are direct access storage devices. In direct access, when data is required from record 596, or it is necessary to change part of that record, the computer can immediately locate the record without reading through all previous records. A computer can then process individual items of data in a direct access system in less than a second where it would take minutes, or perhaps hours, to process them in a sequential system.

The three basic types of direct access storage devices are magnetic drums, disks, and film strips. The magnetic drum looks like a rotating barrel with tracks around its circumference for data recording. Specific tracks on the drum are accessed by a row of read/write heads for recording or retrieving data as the tracks rotate past the head.

The magnetic disk (Fig. 3-16) is similar to a group of phonograph records stacked vertically less than an inch apart. The disk has a group of access arms capable of reading any "groove" or track on any surface. The access arms never touch the disk itself. If they do, they scrape away data and may cause *all* the data on the disk to be lost. Touching is known as a "head crash" and is cause for serious alarm. Some disks are permanently fixed within a housing called a *disk drive,* or *disk unit;* others, called *disk packs,* are removable to increase flexibility. Disks made of flexible material, known as floppy disks, are used for storing comparatively small amounts of data.

Magnetic film strips, such as IBM's data cell and NCR's CRAM, are less commonly used direct access storage media. They use a large number of film strips containing data in magnetized spots. The film strips are held in containers on a rotating carousel (Fig. 3-17). When the desired strip passes the read/write station, it is wrapped around a drum and may be read or written upon.

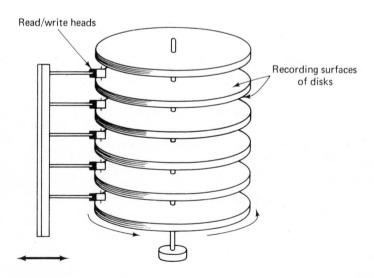

Figure 3-16. The disk concept.

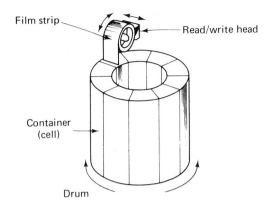

Figure 3-17.　Data cell.

In each of these direct access storage media, data is stored in magnetic spots, usually by means of the EBCDIC code. Each record on a direct access device has an address by which it can be located. Storage capacity of these devices varies from approximately 1 million to 1 billion bytes.

The disk has become the most widely used direct access device. The standard disk of the 1960s was the IBM 1316, a removable disk pack with a maximum capacity of 7.25 million bytes. This device is still widely used today. The 1316 has 10 usable surfaces for recording data, each with 200 usable tracks on it. Each track contains 3625 bytes. Disk packs are often used in clusters; that is, several packs are mounted on disk drives, and their contents are available to the computer. (See Fig. 3-18.)

To locate a specific record on a disk, an input message must contain the record number, also known as a *key*. This key is used to find the address of that record in an index of keys and addresses. An address consists of the disk pack number, surface number, track number, and record number on that track.

Many larger models of disks exist today. A typical large disk facility is the IBM 3300 disk storage. This unit can support up to 16 large disk packs, each with a capacity of 100,000,000 bytes. A larger disk pack, Model 3336, has 19 usable surfaces, each with 400 tracks that can hold 13,000 bytes.

The trend towards storing vast amounts of data directly accessible to a computer has led to the development of various mass storage techniques. Typical of this group is IBM's 3850 mass storage system.

Courtesy of IBM

Figure 3-18. Typical of the high-capacity disk units available today is IBM's Model 3350 direct access device, which houses a series of disk packs.

Data is stored on magnetic tape in fist-sized cartridges, each with a capacity of 50 million characters. The cartridges are housed in honeycomb storage compartments, and when access to data is required, the information is transferred from the cartridge to a disk pack, making it directly accessible to the central processor. With this tape-cartridge-to-disk technique, an organization can have up to 472 billion characters immediately available to the computer. (See Figs. 3-19 and 3-20.)

One disadvantage of disk storage compared with magnetic tape is that, character for character, magnetic tape is much less expensive. A 2400-foot reel of tape costing about $20.00 can easily store 10 million characters, but a disk cartridge for a minicomputer, costing about $85.00, can store only 2.4 million characters.

Courtesy of IBM

Figure 3-19. The two data cartridges shown have a capacity of 100 million bytes of storage, which is also the capacity of the large disk pack in the picture.

Courtesy of IBM

Figure 3-20. Data cartridges stored in an IBM 3850 mass storage system, which can store up to 472 billion characters.

MAKING IT PRACTICAL

Allied Office Equipment is about to put its master inventory file on magnetic tape. The file contains 50,000 200-byte records and will be stored on 2400-foot reels of tape. Allied Office Equipment uses 1600 BPI tape units requiring approximately $\frac{3}{4}$ inch gaps. The systems designer for the project has determined that the blocking factor for the file will be 10 records per block.

How many reels of tape will be required to store the entire file?

The master inventory file of Topping Boots and Luggage has been designed to contain 49 bytes in unpacked form. The systems designers are considering packing the data when storing it on magnetic tape. How many bytes would each record require when packed?

The master record of Topping Boots and Luggage:

Column	Data Field	Type of Field
1–6	Part number	Numeric
8–30	Part description	Alphabetic
31–35	Quantity on hand	Numeric
36–40	Quantity on order	Numeric
41–44	Reorder point	Numeric
45–49	Reorder quanity	Numeric

The master record for students at Harper Valley Junior College contains a field for state abbreviation. When the first three cards in the file were keypunched, they contained NY, OK, and CA, respectively, in this field. Later the cards were converted to a 9-track magnetic tape, which used eight bits for coding in the EBCDIC code. What punches were in the state abbreviation field for each of these records when the data was in punched-card format? What is the bit configuration for these fields on the magnetic tape?

Frugal National Bank is developing a statistical profile of its customers. The file will contain one 70-byte record for each of its 127,000 accounts. The file will be used only once a year when the file is updated and analyzed. You have been assigned to determine the best storage medium for the file.

You have determined that the bank's computer will accept data from any of the basic storage media. You have also ascertained the following capacity and cost figures based on the equipment that the installation is currently using.

Equipment	Cost
80-column punched cards	$1.85 per thousand
2400-foot, 1600 BPI magnetic tape reels containing unblocked records	$20.00 per reel
28-million-byte disk packs	$340.00 per pack

Determine the cost per thousand bytes to store the file. What factors, other than cost, would you consider before making your final recommendation?

REVIEW QUESTIONS

1. Distinguish between internal and external storage media.
2. Explain the difference between direct access and sequential processing.
3. Name three direct access storage devices.
4. Encode JAMES in Hollerith, BCD, and EBCDIC.
5. How does the System/3 card differ from the Hollerith card?
6. What are punched cards primarily used for today?
7. What advantages does magnetic tape have over punched cards as a storage medium?
8. Into how many bytes will an 8-digit number be packed?
9. What is the zoned decimal format? How does it differ from the packed decimal format?
10. Where is punched paper tape used in business today?
11. Compared with punched cards, what advantages and disadvantages does punched paper tape have?
12. How do disks record data? How is data located on a disk?

13. Describe a disk pack.

14. Why are codes used in describing data fields?

15. Why is numeric data more efficient to work with than alphabetic data in computer processing?

GLOSSARY

BCD—Binary Coded Decimal; the coding structure used with several computers, notably IBM System/3

Bit—a binary digit, the smallest unit of storage, which contains either a positive or negative charge

Blocking Factor—the number of records between gaps on magnetic tape

BPI—Bytes Per Inch; the number of bytes that will fit in an inch of tape

Coding—using numbers (or letters) to represent data

CRAM—a direct access device developed by NCR that uses magnetic film strips for recording data

Data Cell—a direct access device developed by IBM that uses magnetic film strips for recording data

Direct Access—the process of locating records in storage without reading through an entire file

EBCDIC—Expanded Binary Coded Decimal Interchange Code; the coding structure used with most modern computers

Hollerith Code—the coding structure used in the 80-column punched card

Interrecord Gap—the space between blocks of records on a reel of tape

Numeric Area—the portion of a byte that contains numeric bits

Packed Decimal Format—an EBCDIC coding structure in which one byte contains two digits

Packing—placing two digits in one byte of storage

Record Length—the number of bytes in a record

Reel Length—the number of feet in a reel of tape

Sequential Processing—processing files that are in numerical (or alphabetical) order

Tape Density—the number of bytes that fit in an inch of tape

Zone Area—the portion of a byte that contains bits for identifying letters or special characters

Zoned Decimal Format—an EBCDIC coding structure for recording letters and unpacked numbers

4

The
Central Processor

Objectives

This chapter explains how the central processor works and how it stores data and programs to produce the results desired by the programmer. The student will also learn the fundamentals of numbering systems and how decimal, binary, and hexadecimal numbers are used in conjunction with computers.

COMPONENTS OF THE CENTRAL PROCESSOR

The essential component of a computer system is the central processor, or central processing unit (CPU). The CPU has three main components: a control unit, an arithmetic-logical unit (ALU), and main, or internal, memory. The control unit and the ALU are electronic circuitry; main memory is often composed of cores that can hold a clockwise or counterclockwise magnetic charge.

The control unit monitors and directs the internal operations of the computer. It receives instructions and analyzes and executes them.

The arithmetic-logical unit is the section of circuitry where the work of the computer is actually done. Numbers are added and subtracted here, and items of data are compared with one another.

Main memory is the section of the central processor that contains the program and the data being worked upon. A normal computer operation stores a program in main memory and then reads individual data records from an input device into a certain area of main memory. The control unit brings a program instruction to the control section and examines it. If an arithmetic or logical function is called for, the control unit finds the required data in main memory, sends it to the arithmetic-logical unit, and instructs the ALU to perform the required work. The control unit then returns the results to main memory, where it is stored, and looks for the next instruction. Time to find, analyze, and execute instructions is measured in billionths of seconds (nanoseconds). Thus, in large computers millions of characters of data are manipulated every second. (See Fig. 4-1.)

ADDRESSING

During normal operations, the main memory of a computer contains programmed instructions and the data currently being worked upon. The control unit interprets each instruction, finds pertinent data from main memory, sees to it that the instructions are carried out in the arithmetic-logical unit, stores the results in main memory, and finds the next instruction. To accomplish this, items in main memory must be locatable. Each byte of storage has an address through which it can be located. Addresses in a central processor's main memory are often described as being similar to mailboxes in a post office. Each box has a number to identify it and identify which items of mail it will receive. In main memory, instructions and data being worked upon are filed electronically. The first storage position, or byte, in main memory is address 000; the next 001, and so forth. Computer storage capacity is measured in terms of how many addressable bytes it contains. A "K" is the standard unit of measurement. Since computer hardware is constructed in base 2 components, a K is actually 1024 bytes (2^{10}). A 64K central processor actually has 64 × 1024, or 65,536, separate addresses for the 65,536 separate bytes.

Each storage position is addressable; the data or instructions that it contains can be located. A nine-position field, such as a social security number, would occupy nine consecutive bytes of storage. Its address in main memory is assigned by the translator program. The programmer merely states that a field called SOCIAL-SECURITY-NUMBER is a nine-byte numeric field. The compiler may assign storage positions 9001 through 9009, or any area it finds convenient, as the location for the social security number field. When the control unit seeks SOCIAL-SECURITY-NUMBER, it will find it beginning at storage location 9001 and will process it according to the programmed instructions.

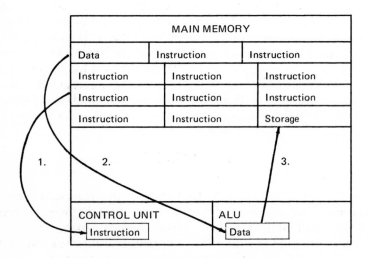

Step 1. An instruction is brought from main memory to the control unit and analyzed.

Step 2. The control unit sends the necessary data to the ALU, and the instruction is carried out.

Step 3. The results of the operation are stored in main memory.

Figure 4-1. The central processor executing a normal instruction.

INSTRUCTIONS

Instructions written in symbolic languages such as COBOL, FOR-
TRAN, RPG, or BASIC are translated into machine-language instructions by the translator program. The machine-language instructions
are then stored in main memory. In simple operations, one data record is read from an input device and also stored in main memory.
The control unit executes every instruction that pertains to that record
and has the result written on an output device. Besides the program
and input data, main memory also contains whatever arithmetic constants are needed for calculations, and storage areas for receiving the
calculation's results.

An ADD instruction might count each record read. In English it
would read:

ADD 1 TO RECORD-COUNT.

"1" is an arithmetic constant stored at a locatable address;
RECORD-COUNT is a storage location used as a work area for accumulating the total. Figure 4-2 shows how main memory looks
when this instruction is being executed.

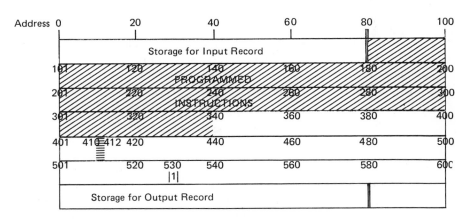

Figure 4-2. In fundamental computer applications, main memory contains
programmed instructions, input and output storage areas for
the current records being processed, work areas for storing
results of arithmetic calculations, and constants required in the
program.

MULTIPROGRAMMING

Today's medium-to-large-scale computers process more than one program at a time. This feature, known as *multiprogramming*, varies with the capacity of the CPU and the computer's operating system. In general, the larger the CPU, the more programs it can handle simultaneously. A CPU with 16K would handle only one program at a time. A 128K model would probably process two or three tasks simultaneously. A super computer, with a CPU of over 1 million bytes, will often execute as many as 15 programs simultaneously.

CHANNELS

The CPU is connected to I/O devices through channels. A channel is a hardware device that regulates the flow of input and output data. When a CPU is multiprogramming, it may be communicating with 20 or 30 I/O devices and perhaps hundreds of teleprocessing terminals. Channels act as middlemen between the CPU and peripheral devices, accepting and sending data to allow the CPU to function in the most efficient way.

MULTIPROCESSING

In large computer installations, CPUs from two or more computer systems are often interconnected. This process, known as multiprocessing, allows more flexible computer scheduling and provides immediate recovery· and continuity of operation in the event of functional failure in one of the computer processors.

INTERNAL STORAGE

Core storage is a common type of device used in main memory. A core is a tiny, doughnut-shaped metal object that can be either positively or negatively charged. Cores receive their magnetism from wires running through them. In many of today's computers, eight cores are strung together to form one storage position, or byte. (See Fig. 4-3.)

Core storage main memory, then, is composed of bytes that store data and instructions. Since each core in a byte can assume only one of two states, positive or negative, on or off, or 1 or 0, computer

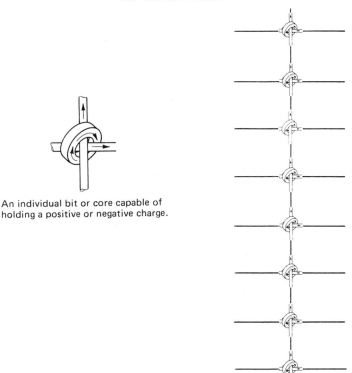

An individual bit or core capable of
holding a positive or negative charge.

**Figure 4-3.   Core storage. In many of today's computers, eight cores are
strung together to form one storage position, or byte.**

instructions and data must be coded in binary numbers when they are
stored internally within the CPU.

Besides magnetic cores, several other types of storage media are
currently used for main computer storage. Solid state, monolithic
circuitry is used in some models of the IBM/370 instead of core storage. The unit of memory, a tiny silicon chip that measures less than $\frac{1}{8}$
inch square, contains over 1400 microscopic circuit elements. The
silicon chips are mounted in memory array modules that store 64
bytes. Monolithic circuit storage requires half the space that core storage requires to store the same amount of instructions.

NCR has marketed a computer system, the NCR Criterion series,
which features a method for making internal storage more flexible.
Microprograms, contained on flexible disks, are loaded into main
memory to improve the ability of the CPU to execute computer languages and specific applications and to expand the potential of the
computer's fixed main memory. (See Figs. 4-4 and 4-5.)

Courtesy of NCR Corporation

Figure 4-4. Instruction sets, known as *firmware*, are loaded by flexible disk into an NCR Criterion 8570 data processing system. These instruction sets alter some of the characteristics of the CPU and provide it with greater flexibility.

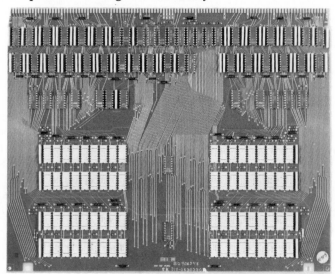

Courtesy of NCR Corporation

Figure 4-5. An instruction storage unit for an NCR computer system. This high-speed memory unit is used to adjust the capabilities of the central processor.

Another concept to expand the capacity of main memory, called *virtual storage,* has become increasingly more important in recent years. Virtual storage permits the central processor to temporarily store instructions that it is not currently using on a direct access storage device on-line with the computer. As instructions are needed, they are brought back into the real, or main, memory, and the instructions that have been executed are sent to the direct access, or virtual storage, area. The real storage areas within the CPU are subdivided into segments called *pages.* A page is only large enough to contain part of a program, so the CPU actually stores parts of many different programs. The remainder of these programs are contained in pages stored on an on-line direct access device. The CPU executes the instructions for the pages that it currently has and continually swaps these pages for the next page in each program to be executed. This entire operation is done by the CPU, with the programmer having no idea of how his program has been divided into pages or where in storage his program is stored and executed.

With virtual storage, large programs can be run in smaller main storage segments, permitting more flexible multiprogramming operations, although at the probable cost of slower overall production. Accessing instructions mechanically from a direct access storage device is slower than accessing them electronically from main storage.

NUMBER SYSTEMS

The binary number system, which uses only two numbers, 1 and 0, lends itself perfectly to computer processing. In order that binary numbers may be better understood, the principles of the decimal system should be reviewed.

All modern numbering systems use position values as the basis for measuring the value of a digit. The further to the left a digit in a number is, the higher is its value. In the base 10 decimal system, the value of each digit is determined by the value of 10 raised to a specific power. Consider the number 675. One automatically says that these three digits equal six hundred seventy-five. But why are they not $6 + 7 + 5$ to equal 18? The reason is that each digit has a different position value. In base 10 arithmetic, the position values are

Base	to infinity	10^3	10^2	10^1	10^0
Position Value		1000	100	10	1

Any number to the zero power is one; a number to the first power is itself, ten squared is one hundred, and ten cubed is one thousand. The values can continue to infinity by adding one to the power and determining a new position value. Thus, 675 equals six hundred seventy-five because:

Base	10^3	10^2	10^1	10^0
Position Value	1000	100	10	1
		6	7	5

$$6 \times 100 = 600$$
$$7 \times 10 = 70$$
$$5 \times 1 = 5$$
$$\overline{}$$
$$675$$

Man uses the base 10 system because it is natural for him to count on his ten fingers and count a large mass of items by using fundamental groups of ten. The computer has no fingers; it can recognize only the two states of on and off, so the binary system was natural for computers.

Base 2 arithmetic works on the same principle of position values used for base 10. In binary, the position values are

Base	2^3	2^2	2^1	2^0
Position Value	8	4	2	1

In the base 10 system, there are 10 digits (0 through 9), and the highest digit is 9. In base 2, there are 2 digits (0 through 1), and the highest is 1. The number 1011 in base 2 equals the number 11 in base 10 because:

Base	2^3	2^2	2^1	2^0
Position Value	8	4	2	1
	1	0	1	1

$$1 \times 8 = 8$$
$$0 \times 4 = 0$$
$$1 \times 2 = 2$$
$$1 \times 1 = 1$$
$$\overline{}$$
$$11$$

What are the decimal equivalents for these binary numbers?

1000	1111
101	1110
11001	11

Convert these decimal numbers to binary.

7	9
10	16
5	1

Computers do arithmetic in binary. Binary addition is shown below. Computers do subtraction, multiplication, and division using similar principles.

Examine these addition examples, remembering that only four possible combinations exist in binary addition.

1	0	0	1
+0	+1	+0	+1
1	1	0	10

Think of the fourth answer as zero and one to carry. What occurred in the fourth example is that one was added to the highest number in the base 2 system, thus requiring a carry. When one is added to the highest number in the decimal system, nine, the result is zero and one to carry (10), also known as ten.

Study this example:

$$10_2$$
$$+ \ 11_2$$
$$101_2$$

To prove the answer, substitute the decimal equivalents of the binary numbers and the problem is 2 plus 3 equals 5.

Another variation is

$$
\begin{array}{rcl}
10101_2 & = & 21_{20} \\
11110_2 & = & 30_{10} \\
\hline
110011_2 & = & 51_{10}
\end{array}
$$

Try these additions:

(a) 1011_2 (b) 111_2 (c) 10101_2 (d) 1101_2
    1110_2 100_2 11100_2 1001_2

What the Computer Does

Did you get these answers?

(a) 11001_2 (b) 1011_2 (c) 110001_2 (d) 10110

HEXADECIMAL NUMBERS

Instructions and data within main memory consist of a string of ones and zeroes. The number +54321 in packed decimal format would look like this in three consecutive bytes:

8		0		0		0
4	(5)	1	(3)	0	(1)	0
2		0		1		0
1		1		1		1
8		0		0		1
4	(4)	1	(2)	0	(+)	1
2		0		1		0
1		0		0		0

Expressed in binary, each byte would be

01010100   00110010   00011100

Since a string of ones and zeroes is difficult to work with, programmers use still another numbering system, hexadecimal (base 16), as a shorthand method of expressing binary numbers. Hexadecimal can express in one digit what requires four in binary.

In base 2, there are two numbers; the highest number is one. In base 10, there are ten numbers; the highest number is nine. In base 16, there are sixteen numbers, the highest having a value of fifteen.

Since a value in a numbering system that is less than the base must be expressed with one digit, ten through fifteen in hexadecimal are represented by A through F. Notice in the table of decimal, binary, and hexadecimal values that a four-digit binary number equals a one-digit hexadecimal number.

Decimal	Binary	Hexadecimal
1	0001	1
2	0010	2
3	0011	3
4	0100	4
5	0101	5
6	0110	6
7	0111	7
8	1000	8
9	1001	9
10	1010	A
11	1011	B
12	1100	C
13	1101	D
14	1110	E
15	1111	F

The advantage of using hexadecimal values may be seen in analyzing the name HUNTER as it appears in core storage in the EBCDIC code. The six bytes contain:

	H	U	N	T	E	R
8	1	1	1	1	1	1
4	1	1	1	1	1	1
2	0	1	0	1	0	0
1	0	0	1	0	0	1
8	1	0	0	0	0	1
4	0	1	1	0	1	0
2	0	0	0	1	0	0
1	0	0	1	1	1	1

The contents of each byte are

	H	U	N	T	E	R
binary	1100 1000	1110 0100	1101 0101	1110 0011	1100 0101	1101 1001
hexadecimal	C8	E4	D5	E3	C5	D9

As a programmer writes instructions, the digits are in decimal form. A valid instruction in the COBOL language would be ADD 3 TO 2 GIVING ANSWER and ANSWER would contain a 5.

The values 3 and 2, which are written by the programmer in decimal, are converted by the computer system to binary format. The computer adds 0011 to 0010, obtaining 0101.

If the programmer was experiencing problems and requested that the contents of main memory be printed out as the program was executing, the arithmetic values would be displayed in hexadecimal notations. The common term for the resulting listing is a "core dump." (See Fig. 4-6.)

MAKING IT PRACTICAL

Gloria Margo has programmed for Spats Shoe Company for five years. During this time Spats has had a 32K third generation small computer that does not have multiprogramming capabilities. Gloria is an excellent programmer, but has always felt confined working with a small computer.

Ms. Margo recently got a job as a programmer at a much larger company, which has a computer with 512K main memory and multiprogramming capabilities. The computer system makes extensive use of virtual storage in its daily operations.

"I've never worked with virtual storage before," she told her new manager, "and I'm a little nervous about working on such a big machine."

What effect do you think the new environment will have on her programming?

REVIEW QUESTIONS

1. Name the three main components of the CPU and tell what each does.
2. Where are binary numbers used in data processing? Where are hexadecimal numbers used?
3. What does the CPU contain when a program is being executed?
4. How are storage addresses assigned?
5. How many bytes of storage does a 32K CPU contain?

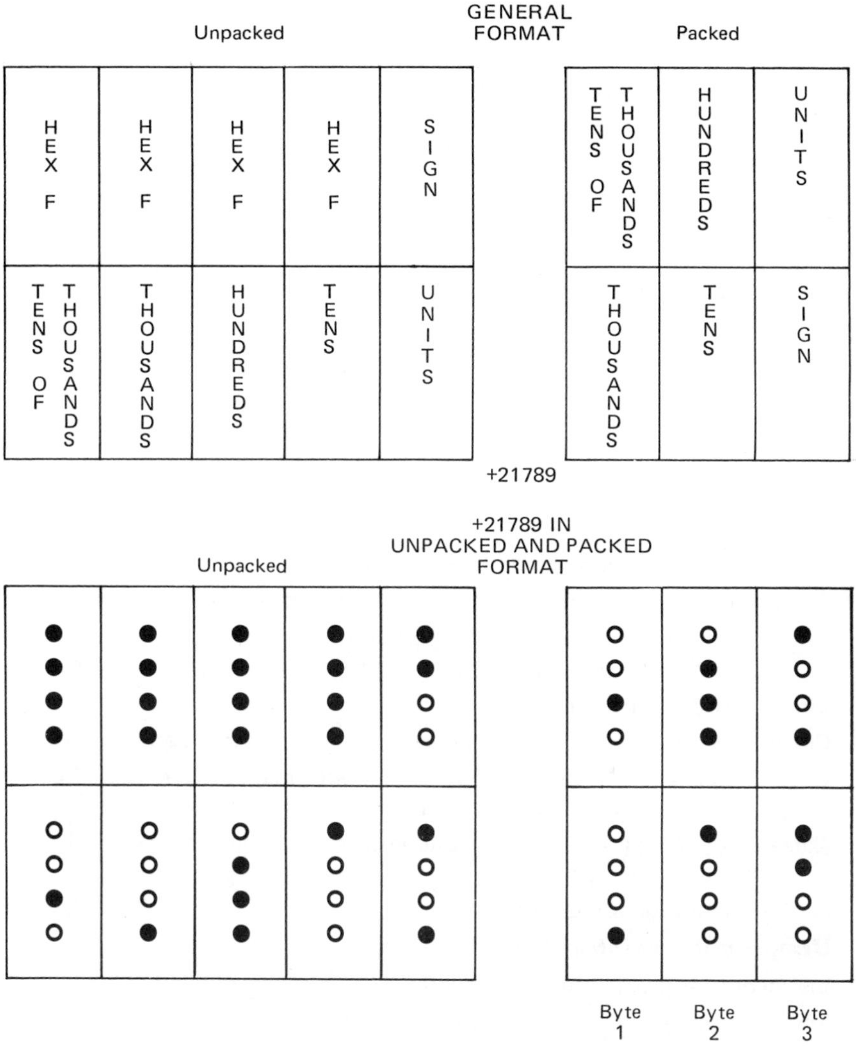

GENERAL
FORMAT

Unpacked					Packed			

Unpacked

HEX F	HEX F	HEX F	HEX F	SIGN
TENS OF THOUSANDS	THOUSANDS	HUNDREDS	TENS	UNITS

Packed

TENS OF THOUSANDS	HUNDREDS	UNITS
THOUSANDS	TENS	SIGN

+21789

+21789 IN
UNPACKED AND PACKED
FORMAT

Unpacked

Byte 1   Byte 2   Byte 3

THE NUMBER +21789 REPRESENTED IN BINARY:

UNPACKED   PACKED
1111 0010| 1111 0001| 1111 0111| 1111 1000| 1100 1001   0010 0001| 0111 1000| 1001 1100

THE NUMBER +21789 REPRESENTED IN HEX:

UNPACKED   PACKED

F2   F1   F7   F8   C9   2 1   7 8   9 C

Figure 4-6.   Computer number representation.

6. Complete the table below:

Binary	Hexadecimal	Decimal
1101010	———————	———————
———————	1A	———————
———————	———————	16

7. Add in binary:

```
11010       111       101010
10101       101       111111
            101
```

GLOSSARY

Address—the number assigned to a location in storage

Arithmetic Constant—a number stored in main memory for use in a program

ALU—Arithmetic Logical Unit; that portion of the central processor where the arithmetic and logical steps of a program are actually performed

Binary—base 2 arithmetic

Channel—a hardware device for regulating the flow of input and output

Control Unit—the circuitry of a central processor that monitors and directs the internal operations of the computer

Core—a tiny, doughtnut-shaped metal object that can be either positively or negatively charged

CPU—central processing unit

Hexadecimal—base 16 arithmetic

Instruction—a programmed command

Multiprocessing—interconnecting two or more CPUs

Nanosecond—a billionth of a second

Page—a segment of the real storage area within a CPU

Real Memory—main memory contained within the CPU

Virtual Memory—a process whereby some instructions of a current program are temporarily stored on a direct access device and called into the CPU when required

II
Processing Data

5

How
Data
Is Processed

Objectives

The chapter illustrates some of the basic ways in which data is processed in business today. The reader will learn how to organize data and how files interact with the computer to produce the information needs of business.

DOING A JOB ON A COMPUTER

Consider that your class was assigned the project of listing pertinent information about every student in the group on a computer. Although listing information about a group this small is more easily done by hand, the class decided to use the computer, because it was planning to do a statistical run later for the entire school. The class is violating the principle established earlier in the text for business data processing applications: Use the computer for high-volume, highly repetitive work. Business data processing usually has large volumes of input and output and comparatively few calculations. Mathematical, scientific, and engineering projects usually have limited input and output, but considerable calculations.

Data for the class listing is gathered with these steps:

1. The group defines what data it wants recorded and listed.
2. A form of appropriate design is composed.
3. The form is presented to each student, who fills in appropriate data about himself. (See Fig. 5-1.)
4. The completed form is keypunched and key verified to record the data in machine-readable form.
5. The resulting data deck, which has one card for each individual, is held until the program is ready.

The program is prepared with these steps:

1. A programmer designs the program and documents its steps in a programming flowchart. A programming flowchart is a graphic outline, or "road map," of the logical steps in a program. (See Fig. 5-2.)
2. Programming instructions are written on special forms called *coding sheets*.
3. The instructions are keypunched and key verified from the coding sheets.
4. The resulting program deck, known as a *source deck*, is in the symbolic language of the programmer, COBOL, RPG, or FORTRAN, for instance.
5. The source deck in symbolic language is translated into an object program in machine language by a compiler program. The compiler, which is located on a disk connected with the computer's central processor, is copied into main memory, and each instruction in the source deck is translated into proper machine-language instructions. The output program in machine language is stored on a disk from which it can be quickly called into the central processor. Once there, it will process the previously prepared data deck to produce the desired output.

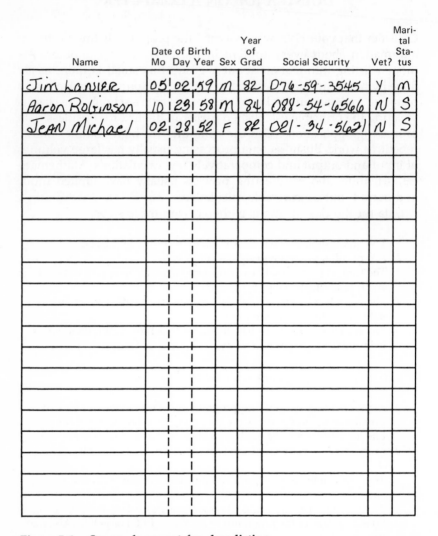

Name	Date of Birth Mo Day Year			Sex	Year of Grad	Social Security	Vet?	Marital Status
Jim Lanier	05	02	59	m	82	D76-59-3545	Y	m
Aaron Robinson	10	29	58	m	84	088-54-6566	N	S
Jean Michael	02	28	52	F	82	021-34-5621	N	S

Figure 5-1. Source document for class listing.

6. The object program from step 5 is called into the central processor and stored.
7. The data deck is then read into the central processor one card at a time. As each card is read, the program processes it and instructs the printer to write one line for each card read.

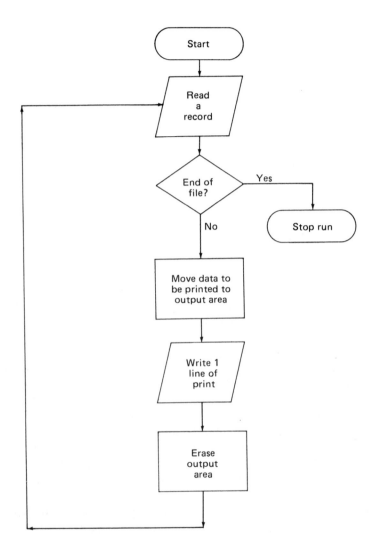

Figure 5-2. A programming flowchart showing the logical steps in a fundamental program.

Figure 5-3 illustrates a systems flowchart showing the steps required to do this simple computer operation.

Although the illustration, a card to printer listing, is the most fundamental data processing application, it contains the steps required to produce the two components of a computer job, data and a program.

Data has several specific classifications; for instance, a character, such as a number, letter, or punctuation mark, is composed of a group of related bits. Groups of related characters are a *field;* groups of related fields are a *record,* and groups of related records are a *file.* Groups of files are often called a *data base* (Fig. 5-4).

UPDATING MAGNETIC TAPE FILES

Files are the basic source of business information, and keeping them current is a major problem in data processing. Two general types of files are master files, which contain the status of a group of records at a specific point in time, and transaction files, which contain changes to master files. Transactions include changes to existing records and records to be added to or deleted from a master file. Updating is the process of applying transactions to an existing master file. A new master file is usually created during the process with the old one retained temporarily.

Punched-card and magnetic tape files are updated through batched input; that is, transactions are accumulated into groups, or batches, and a batch of transactions enters the computer system at one time. The example below illustrates a batched input system:

Dapper Men's Shops is a small retailing chain in the eastern United States. Much of its business is with regular customers who charge purchases. Dapper sends out an itemized billing statement each month specifying unpaid balance, previous balance, and charges and payments transacted during the previous month.

The master file of accounts at Dapper Shops is on magnetic tape. It contains each customer's account number, account balance, and other descriptive information, such as name, address, and credit limits. The file is updated monthly. Each month's transactions are accumulated and batched with adding machine totals taken of them. Transactions include sales on account, sales returns, and receipt of payment from customers. Transaction data, including customer account number, type of transaction, date, and amount of the transaction are keypunched and key verified.

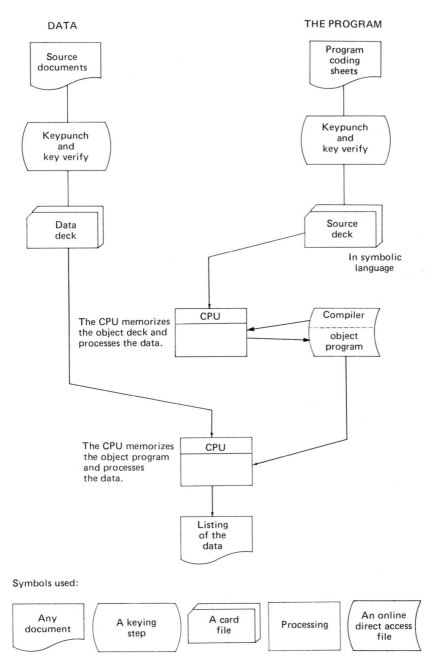

Figure 5-3. A systems flowchart showing the steps required to make a listing on a computer.

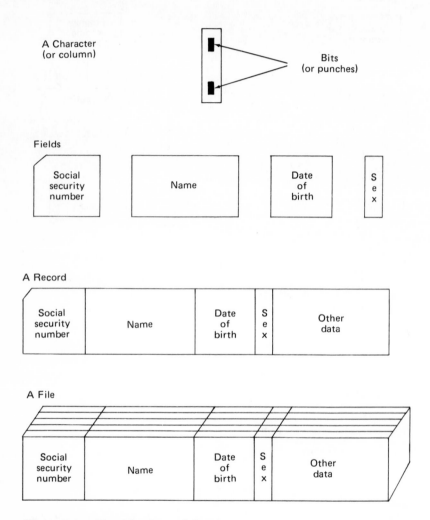

Figure 5-4. Classifications of data.

Magnetic tape files must be processed sequentially. The tape master file at Dapper Men's Shop is in customer account number order. The transaction file must be sorted by customer account number and within that by date of transaction. Magnetic tapes are sorted by computer, a utility program being used. Punched cards are sorted by a card sorter that is off-line, or not connected with the computer system. Each month, both files are brought to the computer for updating. (See Fig. 5-5.)

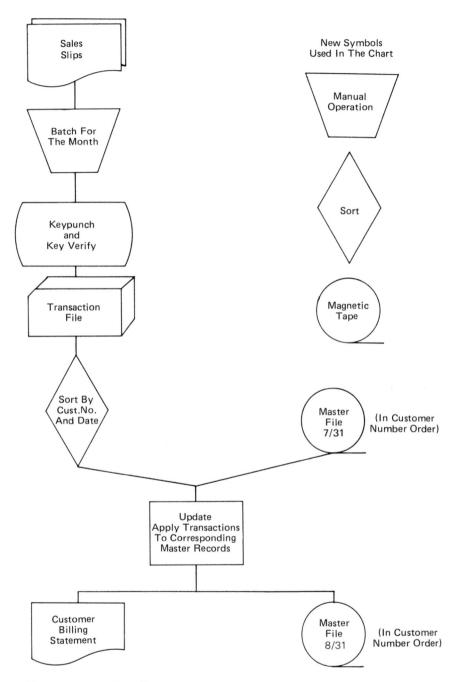

Figure 5-5. A flowchart showing updating of accounts at Dapper Men's Shops.

The updating program first reads the tape master record for each customer and then the transaction records for that customer. Sales amounts are added to the customer balance; cash payments and credit for sales returns are subtracted to calculate new balances. New balances and identifying data are written on an output tape master file, which will be used for next month's updating. The original balance, each transaction for the month, and the new balance for each customer are printed on a billing statement, which is sent to the customer. The transaction file and original tape master file are held temporarily. (See Fig. 5-6.)

DAPPER MENS SHOP
STATEMENT OF ACCOUNT

CUSTOMER:
ROBERT B BRUMEL
43 SECOND LANE
DAYTON OHIO 45479

	DATE	INVOICE NUMBER	QUANTITY	DESCRIPTION	UNIT COST	AMOUNT
PREVIOUS BALANCE	12/31/77					255.00
	1/08/78	1732	2	PR MENS SHOES	8.50	15.00
	1/15/78	1923	12	TIES	6.00	72.00
	1/24/78	PAYMENT				255.00

Figure 5-6. A monthly billing statement.

Dapper Men's Shops is typical of companies that have magnetic tape master files. Some characteristics of tape-oriented systems are

1. They must be processed sequentially. Data records must be in order, usually numerically, occasionally alphabetically.
2. Changes to files are batched, sorted into the same order as the master file, and processed in one pass through the computer. It is impractical to process individual changes to tape master files because an entire new master file must be created.

3. Transactions do not physically change the records on a master file. Updating results in a completely new master file on a different tape.
4. When new tape files are written, their data is usually printed simultaneously, since only machines can read tapes and often people need access to data.
5. It is impractical to look up data about a specific record on magnetic tape. When this type of data is required, the entire file is listed, and clerks look up data contained on the listings.
6. Tape files are constantly checked for existing errors by the programs that process them. When errors are detected, clerks create correcting transactions to maintain the files as accurately as possible.

When tape systems are processed, provision must be made to recover files when they have been destroyed accidentally or lost. Figure 5-7 illustrates a monthly updating system in which both master files and transactions are on magnetic tape. This retention system, known as the *grandfather principle,* provides for keeping master and transaction tapes until three subsequent master files have been produced. This enables an organization to reconstruct a file even when both input and output to a computer updating have been destroyed. (See Fig. 5-7.)

Magnetic tape files may be updated more frequently than monthly, depending upon the organization's information needs. When an organization requires more timely information, direct access equipment must be used.

OFF-LINE PROCESSING

Sometimes it is more efficient to process data off-line, with hardware that is not directly connected with the main computer system. Input data stored on punched cards is usually sorted off-line before being read into a computer system. Scanners often operate off-line by reading data from input documents onto magnetic tape for subsequent processing by the computer. Output files are processed off-line also. Output data is written on magnetic tapes by a large computer, and the data on the tapes is later listed on an off-line printer driven by a small computer. The central processor is then free to do jobs more complex than listing lengthy files.

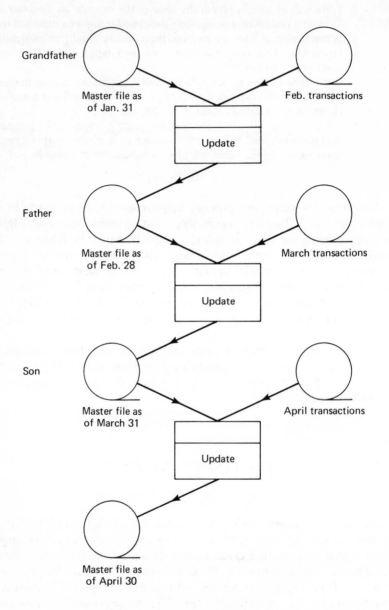

Grandfather

Master file as
of Jan. 31

Feb. transactions

Update

Father

Master file as
of Feb. 28

March transactions

Update

Son

Master file as
of March 31

April transactions

Update

Master file as
of April 30

Figure 5-7. The grandfather principle is used for assuring recovery when a file is damaged or destroyed. Master files and transactions are retained until a fourth generation is produced, at which point the original master tape (now the great grandfather) may be scratched, or used again.

DIRECT ACCESS PROCESSING

Having direct access to specific records permits a radical departure from punched-card and magnetic tape processing. When individual records can be directly accessed, users no longer need lengthy printed reports to locate data. The two breakthroughs in hardware that allowed many separate computer users direct access to common data files were the development of moderately priced direct access storage hardware and teleprocessing equipment and techniques.

The removable disk pack provided flexibility in on-line storage facilities and led to the development of massive storage systems where millions and even billions of characters can be accessed. Systems users reconsidered their processing techniques and began extracting data about specific records rather than constantly printing out entire files. Disk files are accessed not only through messages from hardware located in a computer center, but remotely through teleprocessed messages (Fig. 5-8).

Courtesy of Memorex Corporation

Figure 5-8. A standard disk pack for recording data that can be accessed directly.

Teleprocessing equipment permits an organization to transport encoded data from one location to another, usually over telephone lines. Data is collected from many points, processed by a central computer, and distributed throughout an organization.

In a teleprocessing network, data is converted at the point of origin from its source into electrical impulses, usually by keying. The electrical impulses are carried over telephone lines from the sending station to the receiving station, where they are decoded and either enter a computer system for processing or are displayed on a teletype machine, terminal keyboard, cathode ray tube, or printer. Thus, a teleprocessing network consists of terminals for sending and receiving messages, a carrier, usually telephone lines, for transporting them, and a computer for processing them. (See Fig. 5-9.)

Files are on-line when the data they contain is available to the central processor. Files may be on-line for inquiry, updating, or both. A system that has files on-line for both inquiry and updating and collects data on events as they occur and puts that data to use so quickly that it affects immediately succeeding events is considered a real-time system. A good example of a real-time on-line system is an airline reservations system.

On-line For Inquiry

A paper salesman representing a Chicago firm has almost completed a $10,000 sale to a magazine publisher in Atlanta. Before completing the sale, he keys in the customer's code number and a code requesting credit information at a typewriter terminal located at his branch office in Atlanta. The inquiry is transmitted over telephone lines from Atlanta to the company's computer center in Chicago. The message is received at an I/O message control unit and forwarded to the portion of the central processor's main memory that contains a file inquiry program. The program analyzes the request and locates the customer's record on a disk file on-line with the computer. The record indicates that the customer has a credit limit of $15,000 and currently owes only $3000.

The program receives this information from the disk file and transmits it via the I/O control unit and telephone lines to Atlanta, where the information is printed at the terminal. The entire operation takes a matter of seconds. The sale is completed that afternoon.

In this example, the salesman used a remote terminal and an on-line disk file for inquiry. The system's components included a terminal, telephone lines, an inquiry program located in main memory, an I/O message control unit, and a data file that the central processor could access. (See Fig. 5-10.)

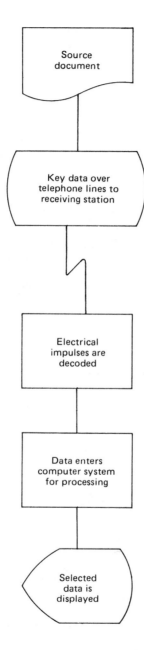

Figure 5-9. Elements of a teleprocessing network.

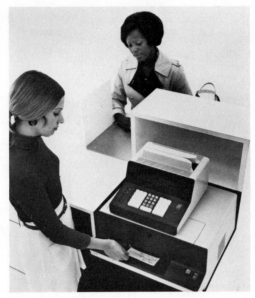

Courtesy of IBM

Figure 5-10. A terminal used for inquiring the account balance of a bank's customer.

On-line For Updating

Hoey Tool Company maintains four manufacturing facilities in Ontario, each more than 100 miles from the main office in Toronto. Hoey's payroll policy is to pay each employee on Friday for the work week beginning on the previous Friday and ending on Thursday. To do this, Hoey uses its teleprocessing network, which links the main office and all the branches. (See Fig. 5-11.)

Data on hours worked is accumulated at each location and keyed into the computer system via terminal on Thursday evenings. This data is stored on a disk file on-line for payroll transactions Thursday evenings. Routine changes to file and data on new employees and employees to be deleted from file update the payroll master file regularly throughout the week. All payroll data is computer-processed Thursday night and payroll checks are run. The checks are delivered by messenger service on Friday in time for distribution before the end of the work day.

This style of processing, known as *remote batched input*, accumulates input at the point of origin and records it in weekly batches. It is used when there is no immediate need to record events as they happen.

Courtesy of IBM

Figure 5-11. **A data entry station online for updating. Sales data is being keyed into a centrally located computer from a sales office.**

Real Time

Quality Auto Parts distributes parts to thousands of auto repair shops throughout the midwestern United States. Quality has fifteen regional warehouses, each of which maintains over 20,000 different automobile parts and accessories in stock. Management at Quality has determined that an immediate and accurate response to customer requests is the most important requirement for success in this business. "Yes, we have that type of tail light in stock." "We have a rebuilt clutch for that model at our Indianapolis facility; we can have it to you tomorrow." is the type of service on which the company is built. To provide this service, Quality has installed a centralized real-time inventory system coordinating the stock in each of its facilities. One large computer holds data that can be shared with and updated by the 15 individual warehouses.

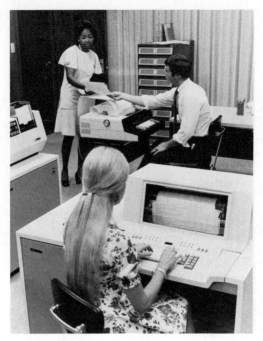

Courtesy of IBM

Figure 5-12.   A teleprocessing terminal with online printer.

Each warehouse is equipped with a sophisticated terminal that has a keyboard for transmitting and receiving messages, a cathode ray tube for displaying the results of file inquiry, and a minicomputer that is programmed to edit transmissions and increase data accuracy. Data on any item placed on order, or received or removed from stock is keyed into the on-line master file as the transaction occurs. Seconds after a transaction has been completed, the current status of the item affected is reflected in the central master file so that when any facility requests stock information, the current status at each location is reported.

The system has provided a substantial decrease in the amount of inventory required to satisfy customer needs, which has resulted in a more profitable investment of capital as well as improved customer service.

Real-time systems provide information on up-to-the-minute status, not the status of the previous day, week, or month. Ordinarily this type of information can be converted to profit by an organization that has sophisticated management.

Time Sharing

In time-sharing computer operations, many users share the same central processor simultaneously. Users may be at different locations within the same company or at different companies. This is possible because a central processor operating at speeds measured in the billionths of seconds can service many I/O devices that process data at a fraction of that speed. While a mathematician at a time-sharing terminal is pausing to consider his next calculation, the central processor has not only solved the problem that he has input, but has gone on to service several other users along the network. In a time-sharing network, the CPU is so fast in comparison with the I/O devices that each user appears to have exclusive use of the computer while in reality hundreds of stations are being serviced at that time. Sharing a computer's central processor is generally more economical than having one's own computer in house for the smaller computer user.

Time sharing is particularly appropriate for scientists and mathematicians whose computer requirements generally have comparatively little input and output but substantial amounts of calculations. In business, many small users who do not have the technical expertise to plan for and program their own computer use time-sharing networks for their routine data processing needs. This type of application uses a more sophisticated terminal for input and output, which would include a card reader and low-speed printer.

Teleprocessing can tie together CPUs as well as I/O devices so that one computer can use the resources of others in the system. This provides backup when one computer malfunctions and leads to an overall workload sharing among the computers. Moreover, files, programs, and data can be exchanged among the branches of an organization.

Time-sharing computer network services may be rented from several large computer organizations. Among the more popular are Control Data's CYBERNET and Computer Science Corporation's IN-FONET.

ORGANIZING DIRECT ACCESS FILES

Direct access files may be organized four different ways: sequential, indexed, random, and unordered.

Sequential

In sequential processing, records are processed on disk similarly to the way in which they are processed on magnetic tape with records placed on the disk in numerical order, one record after another. Ordinarily, files are not stored sequentially on direct access hardware, because it requires rewriting the entire file to update it for changes. Some files that normally would be on magnetic tape may be written on a direct access device to take advantage of the faster processing time a disk provides.

Indexed

Direct access files frequently use indexes for locating records. An index is a cross reference between the identifying number of the record (the key) and the record's address on the hardware device. Some examples of identifying numbers are social security number, customer number, item number, and salesman's number. Software routines are provided to look up the record's address on the hardware from the key in the most efficient way.

Random

Random (or direct) files locate records' addresses by establishing a mathematical relationship between the address and the key. The relationship can be as simple as having the numbering system for items in inventory the same as the disk storage address. More commonly, the address in storage is calculated from the key number by using a mathematical formula called an *algorithm*. The user never knows the storage address of a particular item. The system's software calculates, assigns, and keeps track of all addresses in storage.

Unordered

Traditional data processing uses one file for each application. Accounts receivable has its own file, as does accounts payable, inventory, or any other application. This style of file organization is comparatively easy to work with, but it leads to redundancies in data among the files. If a female employee marries and changes her name, several files may have to be updated.

Today, many organizations integrate all their files into one large data base that is constructed in no specific physical order. Data on two consecutive item numbers in inventory may be thousands of addresses apart in the file.

Software programs, known as *data base management systems,* are designed to access this data and produce meaningful information reports. The key to data base management is that although data is unordered physically, logical relationships exist among data items. A user specifies which items in the data base he wishes to access and the order in which he wants them presented, and the data base management systems programs find the pertinent data and produce the requested report.

Data contained in a data base is structured logically, not physically. Logically related records are connected through links, or pointers, which are fields in a record that contain the address of other related records. Records with similar characteristics have common pointers making them retrievable as a group when requested. Data base management systems may be developed by the user or rented as a software package from one of many vendors in the field.

MAKING IT PRACTICAL

The narratives below describe business situations that may require a change in the basic data processing method. The cases obviously do not contain all the data necessary for decision making, as cost estimates, for example, are not included.

This chapter described seven different ways of doing a job on a computer:

1. Punched card master file—batched input
2. Magnetic tape master file—batched input
3. Direct access master file—batched input
4. On-line for updating
5. On-line for inquiry
6. Real time
7. Time sharing

On the basis of the information contained in the narrative and your knowledge of data processing, which method would you recommend for each of the following?

The county of North Plains is a surburban area just north of a large metropolitan area. North Plains has five cities with populations ranging from 50,000 to 200,000 and an overall population of nearly 1.5 million people. Data processing in the county is decentralized, with each function having its own installation. Functions administered by the county include the central administration, the department of social service, the sheriff's office, the community college, and the county hospital.

The recently elected county administrator feels that so many different computer installations inevitably lead to redundancies in data and inefficiency. In a recent conversation you had with him, he said,

"Social services' computer is always busy. The college's computer is busy during registration, but after that it is just compiling students' programs and doing projects for those egghead professors. The hospital has built its own little kingdom with its computer, the sheriff has his little toy, and I don't know why the computer at central administration is going all day. I do know, though, that I got elected by promising that I would cut government spending, and a county with five computers and five different sets of files and procedures must be doing something wrong."

The county administrator has called upon you to give him some general ideas on how the county can manage its data processing more efficiently. What suggestions do you have for him?

Anderson Associates has just acquired its fifteenth motel in the New England area. The motels, which average 30 units each, are located in the resort areas of Cape Cod and the Vermont ski country.

All of Anderson's data processing is done manually. Each motel operates independently, making a financial report of income and expenses to the main office in Boston monthly. Reservations are handled by mail or phone at each location.

Within the next two years the corporation has plans to acquire approximately 25 more motels in various regions throughout the United States. It currently has no plans for changing its data processing systems.

Do you think that Anderson Associates should consider planning for a computer at this time? If so, what applications can a computer handle for this type of business?

The state of Utiho has a community college system that includes 23 independent campuses. Although student registration is done differently at almost every campus, each location has one common characteristic; it takes an average of three to four hours of standing in line to register every semester.

Of the 23 schools, nine have data processing computers, seven have computers for servicing students mostly in science-related courses, and seven have no computer at all. Of the nine schools with data processing computers, seven use them for registration.

The State Education Department is aware of the problems in registering students and the inconveniences it entails and wishes to do something about it. What suggestions do you have to improve registration data processing in the state?

––––––––––

The city of Fairmont, population 93,000, is located within 25 miles of two large cities. Fairmont statistically has a normal crime rate for an area of its type, which its 150-man police force works hard to control. Chief Tracey has requested that the city install a computer to assist in police work. He feels, "Police work today is largely a matter of collecting data, putting the correct pieces of data together, and providing the proper followup. We can do the followup, but a computer can help us with the first two steps."

What types of data would a police department require? How would you store and retrieve this data? What are some of the sources of input for a police department's data?

REVIEW QUESTIONS

1. What basic principles does the text suggest for determining whether a data processing application should be processed by computer?
2. A computer job requires data and a program. List the steps required to prepare data for a computer.
3. What steps are required to produce a computer program?
4. Explain what takes place when a program is compiled.
5. What is meant by the expression, "Tape files must be processed sequentially"?
6. Explain the concept of updating.
7. Describe a file with which you are familiar that requires updating. How often is it updated? Why is it updated with that frequency?
8. Explain the grandfather principle.
9. Which two hardware breakthroughs permitted direct access processing?
10. Distinguish between on-line and real-time processing.

GLOSSARY

Coding Sheet—specially lined paper for recording programming instructions

Data Base—a group of related files

Direct Processing—random processing; locating data addresses through algorithmic formulas

Field—a group of related characters or columns

File—a group of related records

Grandfather Principle—a record retention system that provides for keeping master and transaction tapes until three subsequent master files have been produced

Object Program—a computer program in machine language

Off-line Processing—processing data with hardware that is not directly connected with a computer

Programming Flowchart—an outline of a program in graphic form

Random Processing—direct processing; locating data addresses through algorithmic formulas

Real Time—processing transactions as they occur so that the master file can provide up-to-the-minute information

Remote Batched Input—accumulating input data at the point of origin for recording in groups, or batches, of transactions

Record—a group of related fields

Source Program—the program as it is written in the language of the programmer

Systems Flowchart—an outline in graphic form of the steps in a system

Teleprocessing—transporting data from one location to another via telephone lines

Transaction File—a file containing pending changes to a master file

Time Sharing—more than one user sharing a central processor

Updating—the process of applying transactions to existing master files

6

Data Recording

Objectives

For over 80 years, the keypunch has been standard for recording data in machine-readable form. Since the mid-1960s, a series of devices has been developed to record machine-readable data in a form other than punched cards. These developments include key-to-tape, key-to-disk, scanners, and terminals. This chapter will explain how data recording devices are currently used for creating computer input.

DATA RECORDING

Data must be converted into machine-readable form before it enters a computer system. Data is originally recorded on forms, such as sales slips, employment applications, receipts, and invoices. These forms are known as *source documents*. Data from source documents is either keyed or scanned to make it machine-compatible. Keyed data is usually stored on punched cards, magnetic tape, punched paper tape, or a direct access device. This data is read by a punched card reader, magnetic tape unit, paper tape reader, or disk unit into a computer system. Scanned data is often recorded on magnetic tape before entering the system. At times, data enters the system directly, as when a teletypewriter or scanner is on-line with a computer system. This chapter discusses keyed input devices, scanners, and terminals.

KEY INPUT DEVICES

Keypunch Devices

The keypunch has been used since Herman Hollerith's day as a method of converting data into machine-readable form. Although it is said that the keypunch is obsolete, keypunch devices are still used in many organizations that use computers.

The keypunch is essentially a typewriter that punches holes in a card instead of printing letters and numbers on a sheet of paper. It has no capital or small letters; its uppercase punches numbers and special characters (numeric mode), and its lowercase punches letters (alphabetic mode). The letters are arranged in a standard typewriter keyboard array, the numbers in the format of a ten-key calculator positioned for punching by the right hand when the machine is in numeric mode. (See Fig. 6-1.)

Eighty-column keypunch devices include the IBM 029 and the UNIVAC 1701. The IBM 029, introduced with System/360 in the mid-1960s, is still widely used for recording data in 80-column cards. The 029 only punches cards; a separate device, the IBM 059 verifier, is required for key verification. The primary limitation of the IBM 029 is in error correction. When an incorrect punch has been made, the card must be removed from the machine and a new card punched with correct data. The 029 can be "programmed" to work more efficiently much as a typewriter uses tab stops. A punched card coded with special controlling punches is wrapped around a program drum and

Figure 6-1. A standard card punch keyboard.

inserted into the machine. The machine is then controlled for punching alphabetic or numeric characters, skipping columns, duplicating fields and filling in leading zeroes.

The UNIVAC 1701 punches and verifies cards. It uses a buffer, or temporary storage unit, for retaining data as it is keyed. When the data for one record has been completely keyed, and the operator feels that it is correct, the data is released from the buffer and the card is punched. When an incorrect key has been struck, the operator need only backspace and key in the correct character. The 1701 can also store programmed instructions for controlling punching. (See Fig. 6-2.)

Many of today's smaller computer systems accept data from 96-column cards. IBM's 5496 Data Recorder, the standard input device with System/3, also uses buffers for temporary data storage during keying and for retaining keying instructions. Decision Data also produces a competitive data recorder for punching 96-column cards.

Keypunching is an economical way of producing machine-readable

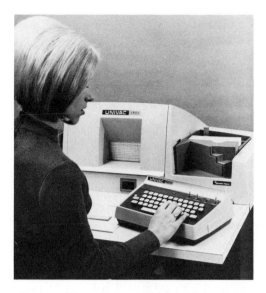

Courtesy of Sperry Univac, a Division of Sperry Rand
Corporation

Figure 6-2. A UNIVAC 1701 verifying punch, upon which both keypunching and key verifying can be performed.

data; keypunch machines rent for from $100 to $175 per month, depending upon the options selected. Keypunches are still popular in business; in fact, most source programs are originally punched on cards. Many businesses have successfully used keypunching for years and are hesitant to convert to one of the more modern data recording devices. Moreover, the punched card is ideally suited for systems that require a manual as well as a machine-readable record. The drawbacks of keypunching devices are numerous:

1. Data in punched cards requires a comparatively slow input device, a card reader, for entering a computer system.
2. Most keypunched data must be key verified. This process, in which all data must be rekeyed to assure accuracy, is literally a duplication of effort. Key verification is usually justified, because it is cheaper to key verify data than to locate and correct errors in data files after they have been processed.
3. Punched-card data must be batched for computer processing.
4. Punched cards must be handled by people, increasing the possibility of error.

Key-to-tape Devices

The development of key-to-tape devices by Mohawk Data Sciences Corporation in the mid-1960s had a serious impact on data input preparation. The original key-to-tape, the Mohawk 6400 Data Recorder, recorded data on a standard 2400-foot reel of tape. This data recorder uses a buffer to facilitate error correction (Fig. 6-3). Honeywell Corporation joined the field in 1968 with the Keytape, yet key-to-tape input did not dominate the data preparation field. Punch cards and keypunching machines were firmly entrenched with users who were experiencing trouble enough converting from one computer to another without adding the complexity of changing data recording devices. Moreover, in large installations with many operators, data was recorded on many different reels of tape, requiring new procedures for sorting and organizing it. Key verifying was still required to assure accuracy, although key verification could be performed on the same device with which the data was punched.

Courtesy of Mohawk Data Sciences Corporation

Figure 6-3. Mohawk data recorder.

Key-to-tape was more widely accepted as it was used with other hardware. The cathode ray tube (CRT), essentially an output device, is used to display data as it is punched. The operator sight-verifies data, reducing the need for key verification. Sight verification requires responsible operators and effective planning in displaying data in easily read format.

Another key-to-tape development was the departure from the clumsy 2400-foot reel of tape to minireels of several hundred feet and tape cassette and cartridge storage for keyed data. IBM's key-to-tape device, Model 50 Data Inscriber, for instance, records data on 100-foot tape reels contained in magnetic tape cartridges. (See Fig. 6-4.)

Groups of key-to-tape devices controlled by a minicomputer are commonly used today. The minicomputer edits and organizes keyed data before it is forwarded to the main computer for processing. These groups of key-to-tape devices, known as *data stations*, often use CRT displays for sight verification. Data is contained on various reel lengths, and the minicomputer is programmed to perform repetitive data recording and editing.

Courtesy of IBM

Figure 6-4. Data cartridge storage for magnetic tape input.

Key-to-disk

The categories of key-to-disk devices include data stations and diskette recorders. A key-to-disk station is a variation of key-to-tape in which data is stored temporarily on disk before being written on magnetic tape. The Honeywell Keyplex System stores data on a disk for up to 64 keyboards.

Courtesy of IBM

Figure 6-5.   In the small computer shown above, both data and programs are contained in small tape cartridges.

The diskette, nicknamed the "floppy disk," is used for recording small amounts of data. Diskettes, which are small, portable, recording devices, are inserted into a recorder, where data is keyed in. When the diskette is removed, its data can be read directly into a computer system. (See Figs. 6-6 and 6-7.)

Courtesy of Datapoint Corporation

Figure 6-6. The Datapoint 100 Diskette data recorder.

Courtesy of Sycor, Inc.

**Figure 6-7.   Data recording on diskette using a Sycor Model 350 intelligent
terminal. A cathode ray tube is used for sight verification. The
station includes a low-speed printer.**

Key To Paper Tape

Punched paper tape storage is appropriate for some systems. Transactions recorded by cash registers and typewriters can simultaneously punch data into paper tape for input into a computer system through a paper tape reader. Punched paper tape is often used for transmitting data to remotely located computers. Teletype Model 33, a paper tape terminal, has long been a standard for creating punched paper tape input. (See Fig. 6-8.)

Courtesy of Teletype Corporation

Figure 6-8.   Teletype Model 33 ASR, a data terminal that reads and writes on punched paper tape.

SCANNERS

Scanners process input data without keying. Data in the format of marks on a sheet of paper or punched card, specially formed alphabetical and numerical characters, or characters formed with magnetically treated ink is read by scanning devices. Four categories of scanners are mark readers, magnetic ink character readers, optical character readers, and data collectors.

Mark Readers

Reading marks from punched cards is one of the oldest means of direct input. Some organizations maintain inventory by recording each sale on pencil-marked punched cards. These sales cards are collected, and the marks are converted to punches by a mark sensor. A more frequent use of mark readers is in test scoring and question-naire evaluation. In some fast food restaurants, the number of items in each sale are pencil marked and read by an electronic calculator for determining price. Mark readers are limited by their lack of precision in reading data (stray pencil marks can be picked up as data) and slow processing rate.

Magnetic Ink Character Readers

Magnetic ink character recognition (MICR) was standardized in banking in the early 1960s. Using a special type font (Fig. 6-9) of numbers and symbols that have been treated with magnetic ink, MICR readers read and sort checks in an off-line operation. An initial sort permits the bank that has received the check to route it to the bank upon which the check is drawn. A second sort arranges the checks by account number for applying the transaction to the individual's account. (See Fig. 6-10.)

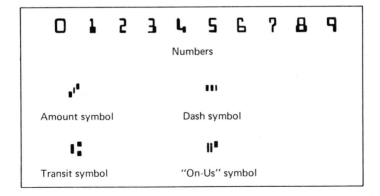

Figure 6-9. The type font used for MICR data representation.

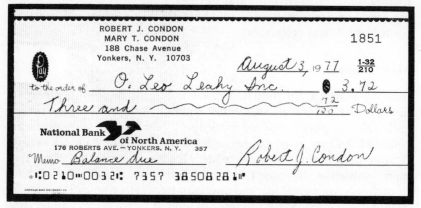

Figure 6-10. A bank check that uses MICR encoding.

Magnetic ink is also used for encoding price tickets on clothing and other retail products. Tickets are encoded for price and item number and become input into a retail organization's regular accounting procedures when the item is sold.

Optical Character Readers

Optical Character Recognition (OCR) refers to those devices that read the shape of characters. Two general classifications of OCR devices are page readers, which read full pages of data, and document readers, which read only one or two lines.

Dozens of different models of OCR devices exist, each with its own capabilities and limitations. Many models read only one type font; others are more flexible. Most read the character's shapes photoelectrically, but other techniques, including laser beam reading, are used.

Ordinarily, data to be scanned is originally created by another machine, such as a computer printer, typewriter, or cash register equipped with a machine-readable type font. Some OCR devices can read handwritten characters as long as these characters are carefully formed and the number of characters per document is limited. Despite the obvious advantage of bypassing the keying step in input preparation, optical scanners have these drawbacks:

1. They are expensive; typical monthly rentals range from $4000 to $20,000. The more flexible font selection, variety of characters capable of being read, and permissible page sizes, the more expensive the hardware.

2. Forms specifications are critical. Forms must be specific lengths, widths, and thicknesses, and must have precise layouts and acceptable quality of ink and printing.
3. OCR devices read input comparatively slowly, varying in speed from 10 to 2400 pages per minute.

OCR devices produce computer input in two ways: off-line, in which data is temporarily stored on punched cards, magnetic tape, or punched paper tape for later computer processing, or on-line, where data directly enters the computer system. (See Fig. 6-11.)

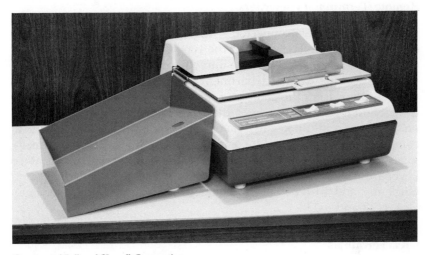

Courtesy of Bell and Howell Corporation

Figure 6-11. **A Bell and Howell MDR document reader, which reads handmade and preprinted marks and holes from punched-card-sized documents.**

Data Collectors

A variety of scanners are also available for collecting data from identification cards, time cards, and credit cards. IBM's System 1030 and Control Data's Transacter systems are leaders in this field.

TERMINALS

Many different types of terminals exist; some are simple typewriters, and others are so complex that they require a computer to monitor them.

The Console

One type of commonly used terminal is the computer typewriter console. A console is merely a typewriter keyboard connected to the central processor through cables usually placed under a false floor. The console is used for inputting limited information and instructions from the computer operator to the central processor. Messages from the CPU are also displayed on the typewriter console.

Remote Terminal Typewriters

Typewriter terminals connected with a computer via telephone lines are very common. The effect of the typewriter terminal is to permit data input from areas not in the immediate vicinity of the computer. Thus a specialist from a department in the same building but on a different floor from the computer can key in data without having to code it and forward it to a keypunch operator. Moreover, a salesman on the west coast can key in data on a sale that he has completed to a computer on the east coast by using telephone lines. Hard copy messages from the computer can be displayed on the terminal's printer-keyboard. Keyboards may be programmed to perform repetitive work efficiently and to type several characters with one keystroke. (See Figs. 6-12 and 6-13.)

CRT Terminals

Terminal input becomes more sophisticated when a cathode ray tube is added to the basic keyboard. The keyboard permits access to the computer and its on-line files; the terminal allows the keyed data and the content of the computer's files to be displayed. The operator can then sight-verify what has been keyed before the data actually enters the computer system. In some instances, data contained on-line is displayed to assist the operator in recording input accurately. For example, an operator may be recording a sale for customer number 2853. The name of that customer may be located in a customer name table on a disk and displayed for the operator on the CRT. The operator then verifies that the name displayed corresponds with the name on the source document in front of him.

Intelligent Terminals

A terminal is "intelligent" when a computer, usually a minicomputer, is part of the terminal hardware. The essential operating difference

Courtesy of IBM

Figure 6-12. A point-of-sale terminal, which checks credit limits before the sale is recorded.

Courtesy of IBM

Figure 6-13. An IBM keyboard display terminal, which is frequently used by bank administrators for fast access to depositors' records.

between intelligent terminals and computer systems is that computer systems process files and intelligent terminals process records. The intelligent terminal's computer is programmed to automate input transactions as much as possible. Calculations are performed, and input data is edited and verified against stored files and tables. For example:

> An operator recording sales on account at a regional sales office keys in a customer's code number and amount of sale. The terminal's computer receives the message and looks up the customer's name, address, and credit limits in an on-line regional customer data file. Name, address, and maximum credit limit are displayed on a cathode ray tube. The operator compares this data with the source document he is using. If it is correct and the sale is within credit limits, the transaction is completed.

Intelligent terminals process data being directly keyed into a system and data that has been keyed off-line and batched, and is being transmitted through a card reader or other input device. Intelligent terminal data entry stations usually include a keyboard, cathode ray tube, low-speed card reader and printer, a minicomputer of perhaps 8K or 16K for storing data processing instructions, and disk storage containing files for supporting the data entry process.

Because they can store instructions, intelligent terminals provide enormous flexibility in the amount and complexity of transactions that they can handle. They can point out errors, validate data, and provide a data entry environment where people, files, and computer interact to provide more precise data. (See Fig. 6-14.)

Specialized Terminals

Certain industries find specific types of terminals suitable for their applications. A bank teller may request an account balance by entering a code and an account number through a Touch-Tone® telephone. A large retailing organization, such as Sears or Korvettes, may input sales transactions through a point-of-sale terminal (POS) operated by a salesperson. Point-of-sale input includes data on retail products encoded with the Universal Products Code (UPC) now seen on most food products, and on specially coded price tags. All terminals serve the same basic purpose; to enter data into a computer system by someone close to the transaction without the added step of coding source data and transporting it to the computer center for key entry. This ultimately reduces clerical errors, simplifies auditing practices, and provides up-to-date data for management decision making. (See Figs. 6-15 and 6-16.)

Courtesy of NCR Corporation

Figure 6-14. An intelligent terminal. This model of the NCR 499 data processing system has a low-speed line printer and a disk storage
capacity of 9.8 million bytes.

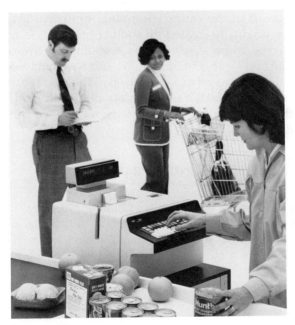

Courtesy of IBM

Figure 6-15. Point-of-sale input being used at a supermarket. The operator
keys in a product code, and the item's price is automatically
retrieved and displayed on a cathode ray tube and on the sales
receipt.

Figure 6-16. **Universal Products Code (UPC) uses bar coding for optical scanning.**

DATA ENTRY TODAY

Data entry in business seems to be in a constant state of change. Today, remote entry through terminals is popular and will be even more widespread in the future. Scanning input, particularly input that has been originally created by another machine, is widely used and will become more significant as scanning hardware becomes more versatile and more economical. We can reasonably expect more imaginative data entry systems to develop in the near future. Still, the vast majority of organizations create data input through key-driven devices with a person converting written data into machine-readable form through keystrokes.

MAKING IT PRACTICAL

Thanks to your help, Pleasant Valley Community College has successfully installed a computer system to maintain its financial records. The college now intends to do grade recording and reporting by computer but has not decided on a basic input method. Three proposals have been made:

Keypunching

Instructors submit a letter grade on a roster sheet, which also contains the name and identification number for each student in the class. Each sheet is keypunched and key verified at the computer center, resulting in one punched card for each course for which a student has registered. The cards are sorted by student identification number on a high-speed sorter (2000 cards per minute). A utility program converts these records to magnetic tape format, which is processed with the student master file to print grade reports. The input grade tape will also update the existing student master file, which contains the students' grades from previous semesters.

Scanning

Instructors submit letter grades by marking the appropriate box with a number 2 pencil on a source document designed for scanning. A scanner reads the student's grade, name, and identification number, which are preprinted on the form, and records them on magnetic tape. The tapes are computer-sorted by student identification number and used to print grade reports and to update the student master file.

Terminal

Instructors hand in roster sheets containing letter grades to their divisional offices. A secretary in each office who has been specially trained for the job keys in the grades for the division at a typewriter terminal. The terminal also has a cathode ray tube for verifying the keyed data. A disk file in the computer center is on-line from nine to five each day for one week after the end of each semester for receiving grade input.

Pleasant Valley currently has or is installing hardware for doing any of the proposals and has a reasonably talented data processing staff which can implement any system. There are 12,000 students currently enrolled at Pleasant Valley.

Write a two-page report on the advantages and disadvantages of each proposal. Specify which system you think will produce the most accurate results and which will produce grade reports the fastest.

REVIEW QUESTIONS

1. What advantages does scanning input data have over keying it?
2. Describe the standard keypunch keyboard.
3. How does the IBM 029 keypunch differ from the UNIVAC 1701 in error correction?
4. List three disadvantages of keypunched input.
5. Comment on the statement, "The keypunch is obsolete."

6. How are cathode ray tubes used with keying devices?
7. What are the advantages and disadvantages of sight verification?
8. How are minicomputers used in input preparation?
9. Name four categories of scanners.
10. List three limitations of optical character readers.
11. Name four general types of terminals.

GLOSSARY

Data Collector—a scanning device for reading data from ID cards, time cards, and credit cards

Diskette—a small portable disk recorder

Document Reader—an optical character reader that reads only a limited number of lines per page

Floppy Disk—a diskette, a small disk made of flexible material

Intelligent Terminal—a terminal that uses a computer for organizing data

Mark Reader—a device for reading data from marks on paper or punched cards

Page Reader—an optical character reader that reads entire pages of data

POS—point of sale; a process in which input data is entered into a computer system by a salesperson

Source Document—the original document from which input data is taken

Tape Cartridge—a container for small reels of magnetic tape

UPC—Universal Products Code; a bar code for scanning data on consumer products

7

Computer Output

Objectives

Results of computer processing are either stored for further computer processing or displayed for the users' information. This chapter will explain how computer output is produced and how it is used by man and machine to fulfill the needs of the business community.

TYPES OF OUTPUT

Computer output serves two purposes: some output is read again by computers, other output is read by man.

Output for machine use is stored on punched cards, punched paper tape, magnetic tape, and direct access storage devices. Output media for man's use include printers, plotters, terminals, and microfilm. In some instances, output is printed with special type fonts so that man can process it and reenter it into the computer system.

OUTPUT FOR MACHINE USE

When computers first became popular, data files were maintained on punched cards. The advantages of magnetic tape over punched cards as a storage medium soon became apparent and limited the use of punched cards for output data storage. The primary disadvantage of punched-card computer output is that card punch devices are slow. Speeds as low as 300 cards per minute are considered fast for card punching but intolerably slow for most data processing needs. Most computer systems today still use some limited card punching. In large systems, punched cards are used when small amounts of output are required and the printer is occupied with other tasks. Errors in input data detected by a program may be punched onto cards and subsequently listed. Summary and control totals may also be punched and later listed when it is not convenient to list them immediately on a printer. (See Fig. 7-1.)

Punched card output files are used today in low-volume operations with small computers. The 96-column card used with IBM System/3 is frequently used for storing master file data.

Magnetic tape is frequently used for recording output data that will eventually be used again by computer. Storing data on tape has two advantages: It can be read rapidly by a computer system, and byte-for-byte magnetic tape is the most economical storage medium. Tape libraries, like the one in Fig. 7-2, efficiently store the data required to run any business. Magnetic tape is used to store data temporarily as well as permanently. For example, many programs require two printed output files when only one printer is available. In this instance, while one file is printed, the other is simultaneously written on magnetic tape and later printed off-line. (See Fig. 7-3.)

Courtesy of IBM

Figure 7-1. From left to right, a card reader, a card punch, and a keyboard-printer terminal. Collectively they are known as the IBM 3770 data communications system, a general-purpose terminal for a teleprocessing network.

Courtesy of IBM

Figure 7-2. Files for large organizations are often stored in magnetic tape data libraries.

Courtesy of Telex Corporation

Figure 7-3.   A magnetic tape unit.

Writing on magnetic tape destroys the data that the tape previously contained. To minimize the possibility of accidentally destroying vital records, an operator is required to insert a file protection ring on the tape before data writing can begin (Fig. 7-4).

Direct access storage devices are frequently used for storing computer output. When data is written on these devices it is immediately available to the computer system's users. For example, an updated inventory file on a disk pack can be searched for the balance of any item in stock by anyone having access to the file through a terminal. When this type of information is required, the additional cost of storage on disk is more than compensated for by the accessibility of the data.

Punched paper tape also stores computer output data that can be reintroduced into a computer system, although punched paper tape is usually restricted to specialized uses in current operations.

Courtesy of IBM

Figure 7-4.　A file protection ring must be inserted in a tape spool before writing can take place.

DISPLAYING COMPUTER OUTPUT FOR MAN'S USE

Many devices display computer output for man to interpret. Printers write output on paper; terminals type output or display it on cathode ray tubes. Output is printed, graphic, or audio. It can be in complete detail, summarized, or selected.

PRINTED OUTPUT

For the past 30 years, most computer output for man's use has been printed. When IBM developed its second generation 1401 computer in the 1950s, it supported it with the IBM 1403 high-speed printer for displaying files and selected output. Updated models of the 1403 are still widely used as are a variety of other high speed printers. Printer output is in three formats:

- detailed—A line of print results from each record processed.
- summary—Totals for groups of records are printed.
- selected—Contents of specific records are displayed.

Printers are used extensively for displaying data from punched card and magnetic files. Man can effectively use punched card or magnetic files only after regular reports have been printed from these files.

Detailed reports of master files are voluminous and difficult to handle. For example, an inventory file for 40,000 parts would require at least 40,000 lines of print. To use this report, the user must consult this stack of paper whenever questions about specific items in inventory arise. Detailed printing of files is used when the files are small, when permanent hard-copy records are required, or when staff members require detailed information in conducting day-to-day business. But an organization runs the risk of drowning in its own paperwork when many large-volume magnetic or punched-card files are detail-printed.

Summarized reports are widely used by middle and upper management in routine decision making because the reports are more concise and easier to handle. Payroll might be summarized by gross pay for each department; a sales file by monthly sales for department or division. Summarized reports often include year-to-date data or comparisons of current data with comparable data from previous periods.

Reports of selected data are used to pinpoint specific problems and initiate remedial action. Some typical reports are a listing of all salesmen who did not meet quota during the past month, all accounts receivable in excess of $1000, all invoices payable that are past due, or all employees who are over 62 years of age.

PRINTER HARDWARE

Two general classifications for printers are impact and nonimpact. In impact printers, printing is caused by a character striking paper through an inked ribbon. The workhorse impact printer has been the IBM 1403. It has character sets located on a rotating chain that works similarly to a bicycle chain. When the letter to be printed passes the desired print position, the character contacts the paper through an inked ribbon and is printed. Chain printers print one character at a time. Models of the IBM 1403 normally print 132 characters per line and 1100 lines per minute (Fig. 7-5).

Many other printers use a rotating set of drums for printing lines. Drum printers contain one drum for each print position. Each drum rotates to the character to be printed at that print position. When a line of print is set up, the entire line is impacted simultaneously. Drum printers typically print 1400 lines per minute.

Nonimpact printers use several different printing principles, including laser beams. These printers are generally much faster than impact printers; speeds of up to 25,000 lines per minute are attainable,

Courtesy of IBM

Figure 7-5.   IBM 1403 printer.

but are only feasible in organizations that have unusually complex printing requirements.

Because data can be written much faster on magnetic tape than on a printer, much printing is done off-line after a file has been originally written on tape. Whenever possible, organizations avoid listing an entire file on a printer, because it is a relatively slow output device. (See Figs. 7-6 and 7-7.)

OTHER OUTPUT DEVICES

Graphic displays of computer-processed data are common in scientific and engineering computer applications and are becoming increasingly popular in business data processing. A plotter converts mathematical values to graphic coordinates and displays them on a cathode ray tube or paper. Graphs for sales forecasting can be visually displayed for management and altered or updated by keying in more recent data. (See Figs. 7-8 and 7-9.)

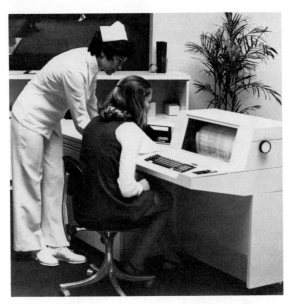

Figure 7-6.   A computer prints a patient's billing charges at a hospital's discharging office.

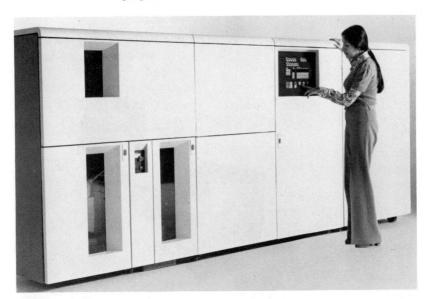

Figure 7-7.   IBM 3800 printing subsystem, which uses laser technology to produce reports at a speed of up to 13,000 lines per minute.

Figure 7-8. A Calcomp 960 plotter for graphic display of computer output.

Figure 7-9. A terminal using a cathode ray tube for graphic output.

Matrix Displays

Computer output in matrix form is seen most frequently in scoreboard displays at athletic events, where numbers and designs are formed to display computer-generated data (Fig. 7-10). Matrix displays are being used increasingly in business, especially for informing large groups of people of the results of computer processing.

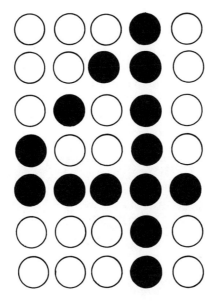

Figure 7-10. Matrix printing for the figure 4.

Microfilm

Computer output microfilm (COM) is used for storing large amounts of data. Microfilm stores data more efficiently than paper. Data can be microfilmed as it is displayed on a CRT or after it is written on magnetic tape. In both methods data is recorded faster than with printing, frequently as much as ten times faster.

Microfilm output has limited application. To consider COM, an organization must meet these requirements: There must be large volume of output, the output must be referenced by man, and it must be stored relatively permanently. COM requires a large equipment investment—recorders, developers, duplicators, and film readers—to produce output that will not be read again by computers.

Terminals

Three general types of terminals for displaying output data are type-writer terminals, CRTs, and audio response.

Since typing is slow (10 to 14 characters per second is normal), typewriter terminal output is used when small amounts of output data are displayed. It is most effective in printing the answer to inquiries of on-line files or a mathematical problem that has been keyed in at a terminal.

CRT displays are more expensive, but display more data in a format more readily understood by the user. CRT terminals are commonly used in the offices of executives to keep them current on the changing picture of a company's activities as reflected in its on-line files. Perhaps the strongest trend in output processing today is the growing use of CRT displays as a means of querying the status of specific records in file and displaying it so that the system's users can take immediate action. (See Fig. 7-11.)

Courtesy of Sperry Univac, a division of Sperry Rand Corporation

Figure 7-11.   Computer output display at a terminal located in the computer center. The computer pictured is a Sperry Univac 1100.

Audio response, where output is verbal, has limited use currently. Audio response requires translating output data into a prerecorded vocabulary. The verbal response is then transmitted over telephone lines to where the inquiry was made.

Business is continually reassessing its information needs, and the trend today is to display specific, pertinent data items at the location where they are immediately required. This demands up-to-date, on-line files and output displays designed for people's needs. (See Fig. 7-12.)

Courtesy of IBM

Figure 7-12.   An IBM System/370 Model 115. The device in the foreground is an IBM 3450 Diskette input/output unit, which replaces a card reader and a card punch.

MAKING IT PRACTICAL

Capital City has a population of nearly 750,000 and is located within 100 miles of several large cities in the eastern United States. It has typical large-city problems: an extensive area in need of renewal that is prone to fires, a relatively high crime rate, and a tight budget for public safety.

Capital City has decided to install a medium-sized computer for the exclusive use of its fire and police departments. The municipality's policy is to use the computer primarily for the safety and well-being of the public.

The city is still planning how to use the computer, but some of the proposed applications include:

1. Allocation of fire-fighting equipment and personnel for maximum coverage in peak times and in high-risk areas. The computer also is envisioned as a communication link between men at a fire site and data and expertise located at headquarters.
2. Planning the location of future fire and police facilities.
3. A source of information for police officers in patrol cars who are conducting investigations. The department is currently troubled by unauthorized intercepts of its voice communications and hopes to solve this problem through coded computer output. It is also planned to link Capital City's computer system with those of other police departments and with the state motor vehicle department.

As yet, the systems planners have not decided how to get the information from the computer to the firemen and policemen in the field. Various output media have been discussed, but no conclusions have been drawn. What suggestions do you have for the planners?

REVIEW QUESTIONS

1. Where is computer output on punched cards used today?
2. What advantages does magnetic tape have as an output storage medium?
3. Distinguish between detailed, summary, and selected reports.
4. Comment on this statement: "Printers that print faster than 10,000 lines per minute are only going to cause an organization to drown in its own paperwork."
5. Why is much printing done off-line?

6. Microfilm certainly stores data efficiently. Why do not all large companies use it for storing output files?

7. Give five examples of instances when cathode ray tubes may be used for displaying data.

8. Comment on this statement: "We don't print reports anymore; we just display the information we need."

9. Many computer operators use the phrase, "No ring, no write." What do you think this means?

10. List three applications in which you think that output on a plotter would be helpful.

GLOSSARY

COM—Computer Output Microfilm; storing data files on microfilm

Detailed Output—a report that prints one line of print for every record read

File Protection Ring—the ring that must be inserted in a reel of magnetic tape before writing can take place

Plotter—a graphic display of computer output

Selected Output—a report on specific items in a file

Summary Output—a report containing totals for groups of records

III
Programming

8

An Introduction to Programming

Objectives

Since every task the computer performs is programmed, a general idea of how programming is performed is essential for understanding computer processing. This chapter and the following two are not intended to develop programmers. Instead, the reader should concentrate on how business tasks are converted to sets of programming instructions. Ultimately, he will be able to communicate better with data processing professionals when he has a clearer understanding of their roles and problems.

PROGRAMMING LANGUAGES

Dozens of different programming languages exist, each designed to make it easier for people to communicate with the computer system. Almost all programming languages are symbolic, created to make programming easier for the programmer. COBOL, FORTRAN, and RPG are symbolic languages, each designed to satisfy a special need of programmers. Each computer model has its own machine language, the only language with which the computer can work. Translator programs convert symbolic language instructions into all-numeric machine language.

A COBOL source program that runs on an IBM computer can fairly easily be used on a Burroughs computer, but the object program—the program in machine language after it has been translated—will not execute on the Burroughs. A translation from the COBOL source program to the Burroughs machine language is required.

Symbolic languages are classified as low level and high level. A low-level language, such as Basic Assembler Language, is structurally close to machine language. The format of high-level languages, COBOL and RPG, for example, is quite different from machine language. Higher-level languages are easier for a programmer to learn but require more sophisticated translator programs. Lower-level languages are difficult to learn, but their translator programs are not so complex.

Two types of translator programs are assemblers, which translate instructions item for item, and compilers, in which more than one machine language instruction may be generated from each symbolic instruction.

STEPS IN WRITING A PROGRAM

Each of these general steps is done in programming writing:

1. Define the problem.
2. Specify the input and output files and hardware devices.
3. Flowchart the solution.
4. Code the solution in symbolic language.
5. Keypunch the program to create the source deck.
6. Have the computer translate the source deck into an object program.

7. Test the object program with small amounts of specially prepared data.
8. "Debug" the program.
9. Complete programming documentation.
10. Turn the program over to the operating staff who will run it on a regular basis.

These ten steps are explained below.

Problem definition is the joint responsibility of the programmer and the systems analyst. A systems analyst is a data processing professional who examines business problems and formulates solutions to them. Too often, programmers invest time in writing programs that are not what the users anticipate. Before a program is written, the programming objectives should be written and reviewed by everyone affected by the program. When objectives are agreed upon, the systems analyst and programmer document the program's prospective output and circulate it for review. When it is approved, input data formats are finalized and programming begins.

The required programming instructions are outlined in a programming flowchart, or block diagram. At first, the programmer draws a general flowchart specifying the general routines that the program will contain (Fig. 8-1). This is later refined into a detailed flowchart depicting each step that the computer must follow to produce the desired results (Fig. 8-2).

The solution is coded in a symbolic language on a coding sheet. Coding consists of describing the files and records that will be used with the program and specifying the programming steps required to do the job (Fig. 8-3).

The coded program is keypunched and often key verified, the programming steps being thus converted to machine-readable form. The punched deck of cards, known as the source program, is taken to the computer and translated by the compiler into an object program in machine language. Programs do not always translate correctly during the first compilation. Programmers often make grammatical errors or attempt steps that violate the basic structure of the language. These mistakes are detected by the compiler, which prints a listing of errors known as a *diagnostic listing* (Fig. 8-4). The compiler can detect only grammatical or structural errors. Logical errors that result in incorrect output but do not violate the rules of the programming language cannot be detected by a compiler. A programmer analyzes the diagnostic listing, keypunches corrections, and resubmits the program until he has an error-free compile.

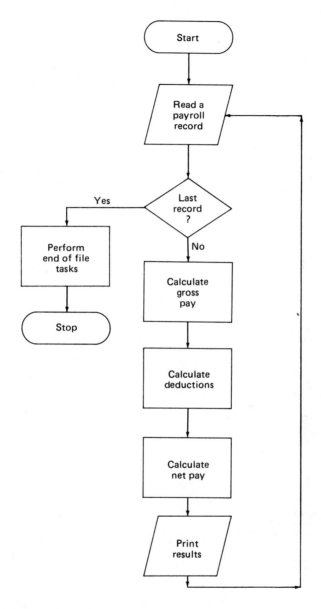

Figure 8-1. A general flowchart for calculating net pay.

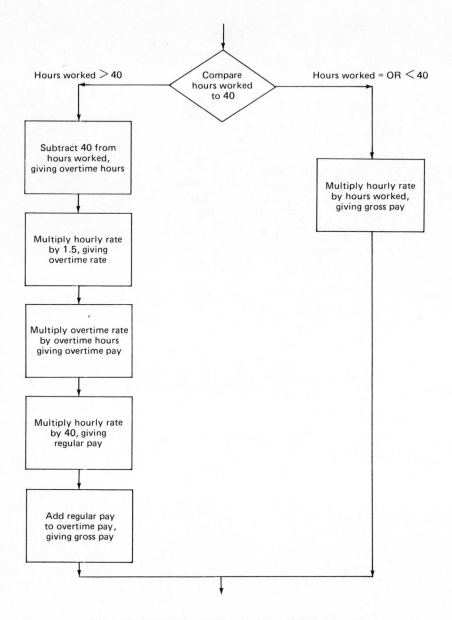

Figure 8-2. A detailed flowchart showing the calculating of gross pay. These steps were contained in one symbol in the general flowchart.

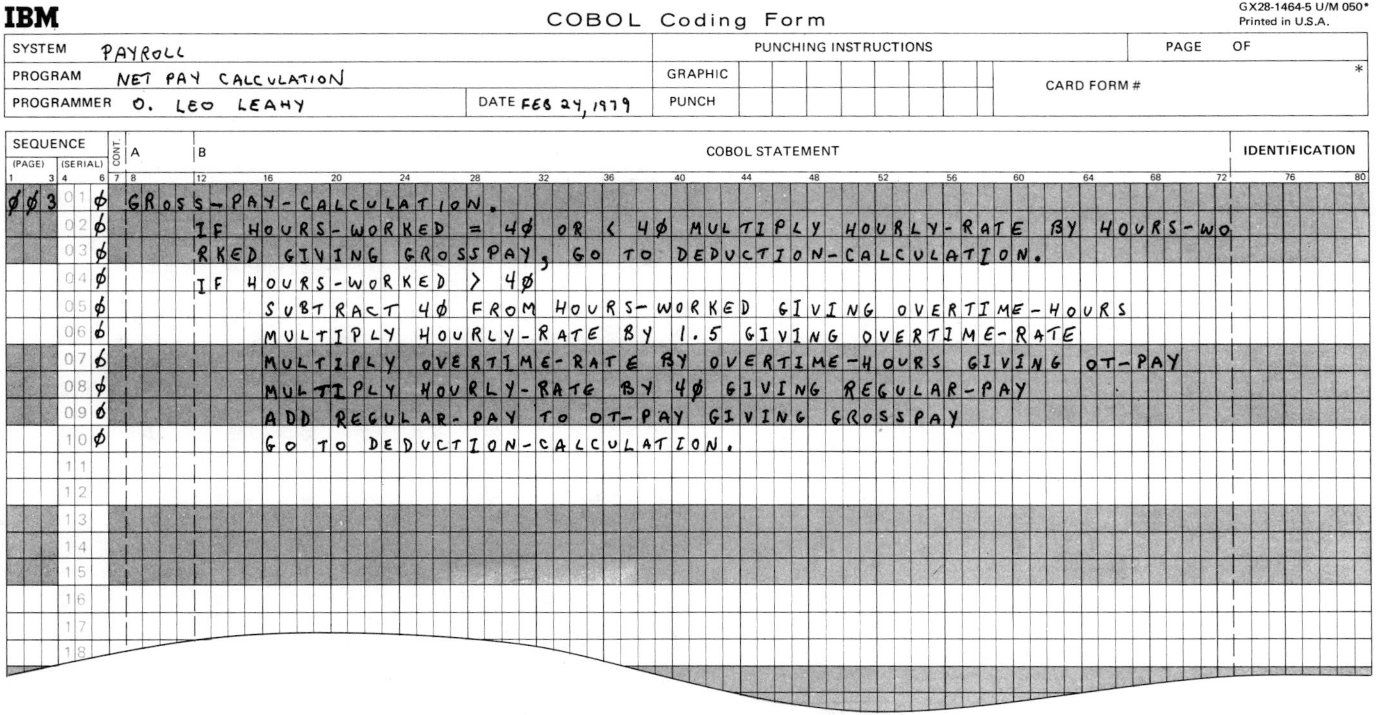

COBOL Coding Form

GX28-1464-5 U/M 050*
Printed in U.S.A.

SYSTEM	PAYROLL		PUNCHING INSTRUCTIONS		PAGE	OF
PROGRAM	NET PAY CALCULATION		GRAPHIC			*
PROGRAMMER	O. LEO LEAHY	DATE FEB 24, 1979	PUNCH	CARD FORM #		

SEQUENCE (PAGE) (SERIAL)	CONT.	A	B	COBOL STATEMENT	IDENTIFICATION
∅∅3 01	∅	GROSS-PAY-CALCULATION.			
02	∅	IF HOURS-WORKED = 4∅ OR (4∅ MULTIPLY HOURLY-RATE BY HOURS-WO			
03	∅	RKED GIVING GROSSPAY) GO TO DEDUCTION-CALCULATION.			
04	∅	IF HOURS-WORKED > 4∅			
05	∅	SUBTRACT 4∅ FROM HOURS-WORKED GIVING OVERTIME-HOURS			
06	∅	MULTIPLY HOURLY-RATE BY 1.5 GIVING OVERTIME-RATE			
07	∅	MULTIPLY OVERTIME-RATE BY OVERTIME-HOURS GIVING OT-PAY			
08	∅	MULTIPLY HOURLY-RATE BY 4∅ GIVING REGULAR-PAY			
09	∅	ADD REGULAR-PAY TO OT-PAY GIVING GROSSPAY			
10	∅	GO TO DEDUCTION-CALCULATION.			

Figure 8-3. A coding sheet showing net pay calculation in COBOL.

| V46B | COBOL COMPILATION | | WCCC | DIAGNOSTIC LISTING |

MSG INDEX	SOURCE SEQ.NO	SEVERITY CODE	ERROR MESSAGES
71126	00074	2	MARGIN A VIOLATION OR INVALID WORD APPEARS ON THIS LINE.
71125	00075	1	INVALID WORD FOLLOWING PARAGRAPH-NAME.
71174	00082	2	PERIOD MISSING OR INVALID WORD APPEARING ON THIS LINE.

TOTAL	00003	STATEMENTS IN THIS DIAGNOSTIC LISTING.
	00001	IN SEVERITY CODE 1.
	00002	IN SEVERITY CODE 2.

Figure 8-4. A diagnostic listing from a COBOL compiler.

An error-free compile means that the program does not contain structural errors, but it still may contain logical errors. There is no way that a compiler can detect that a programmer added deductions to gross pay when he intended to subtract them. The object program then is tested with sample data to see whether it is accomplishing what it is designed to do. Program testing is challenging, because a programmer must anticipate everything that can possibly go wrong with a program presently and in the foreseeable future, both in terms of incorrect input data, such as a letter in a social security number field, and operator mistakes, such as using the wrong tape reel. This anticipation often taxes a programmer's ingenuity.

When the program tests satisfactorily, the programmer completes the program's documentation. This includes a flowchart of the final version of the program, layouts of input and output, a listing of the errors the program detects and instructions on how to handle them, and specific instructions for the operating department on how to run the program. The program and its documentation are turned over to the operations department when the entire system is ready. If programming is properly done, the operating department may use the program for several years before revision is necessary.

Change is inevitable in business, and as conditions change, program modification is required. Routine programming maintenance is essential. It is facilitated when a program is properly documented, because often the person who writes a program is not around several years later, when changes must be made by someone else.

PROGRAMMING INSTRUCTIONS

A program consists of two general areas—file and record descriptions, and instructions. File and record descriptions are handled differently with each symbolic language and are discussed later.

Programming instructions are written in symbolic language and translated into machine language. In machine language, most instructions have these two functions:

Operation Code   a command to the computer to carry out a particular step

Operands   addresses in storage where data being worked upon is
                   stored and may be located

Examine this simple ADD instruction written in COBOL.

ADD WEEKLY-PAY TO YEAR-TO-DATE-PAY

This symbolic instruction must be translated into machine language before the computer can carry it out. The verb, or command, ADD is converted by the computer to a number, which we will represent in hexadecimal. The hexadecimal number FA is the machine language command or operation code for ADD in IBM/360 machine language. The symbolic terms WEEKLY-PAY and YEAR-TO-DATE-PAY represent storage addresses where the data to be worked with is located. They are the operands of this instruction. The storage addresses for these symbolic names were assigned by the compiler, and the addresses and field lengths are retained in the object program. The instruction literally means

ADD THE CONTENTS OF THE STORAGE LOCATION CALLED WEEKLY-PAY TO THE CONTENTS OF THE STORAGE LOCATION CALLED YEAR-TO-DATE-PAY AND STORE THE SUM IN YEAR-TO-DATE-PAY.

When converted to IBM/360 machine language, the instruction might read:

Operation Code	Field Lengths		First Address	Second Address
FA	3	5	2400	1234

which means:

ADD THE CONTENTS OF A 3 BYTE FIELD LOCATED BEGINNING AT ADDRESS 2400 TO THE CONTENTS OF A 5 BYTE FIELD LOCATED AT ADDRESS 1234. (See Fig. 8-5.)

Other instructions, such as subtract, move, and compare data, operate similarly. Symbolic instructions like READ and WRITE are macro instructions. Macro instructions create a series of machine language instructions with one symbolic one.

The illustration above shows one example of how a compiler translates from symbolic to machine language. Notice two of the functions a compiler performs:

- First, the compiler converts what is convenient for the programmer to express (symbolic)

ADD WEEKLY-PAY TO YEAR-TO-DATE-PAY.

to what the computer can work with (machine language).

FA3524001234

- Second, the compiler assigns addresses in main storage for each of the symbolic names in the program.

Notice also that the machine-language instruction FA3524001234 is expressed with hexadecimal numbers. The instruction is actually stored within the central processor's main memory with a string of ons and offs, or ones and zeroes, as seen in Fig. 8-6.

PROGRAM CONSTRUCTION

A program is a series of instructions similar to the one illustrated above. When the instructions are in proper sequence, they achieve the objectives of the program.

Elementary data processing programs follow this format:

- Read a record.
- Process it.
- Write the results of the processing.
- Read the next record.

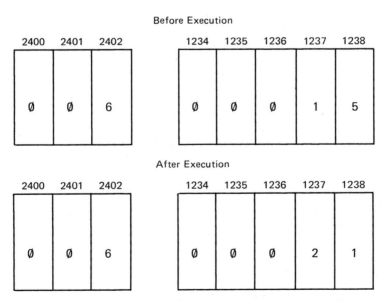

Figure 8-5. Storage contents of the 3-byte field at location 2400 and the 5-byte field at location 1234 before and after an ADD instruction is executed.

	Operation Code	Length Codes	1st Operand (Address)	2nd Operand (Address)
Hexadecimal	FA	3 5	2 4 0 0	1 2 3 4
Binary	1111 1010	0011 0101	0010 0100 000000000	0001 0010 0011 0100

6 Bytes

**Figure 8-6.   The ADD instruction illustrated in this chapter expressed in
hexadecimal requires six bytes of storage. The binary numbers
show exactly what each byte of storage contains. You can see
how the hexadecimal numbers represent the data more clearly
to a programmer.**

This sequence continues until all records have been processed, at
which time routines for end of file are performed (Fig. 8-7).

As programs become more complex, this simple circle or loop is
continually broken as the program performs different routines when
required. The programmer instructs the computer to execute various

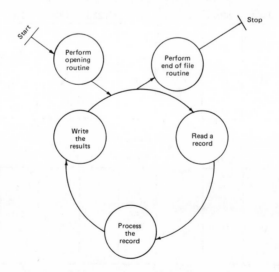

**Figure 8-7.   An elementary program is like a circle. It keeps returning to its
starting point until all the records have been processed. Then it
performs end-of-file routines and stops.**

routines depending upon the results of tests, such as whether a person has worked more than 40 hours in a week, that are built into the program. The programmer specifies what part of the program the computer must execute and where to return when the routine has been completed (Fig. 8-8).

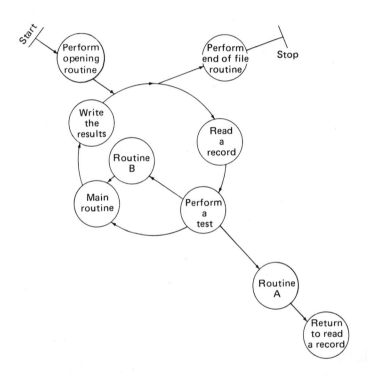

Figure 8-8. **A slightly more complex program, in which different routines are performed depending on a test.**

The use of literals, labels, routines, branches, and loops are among the standard techniques used by programmers.

A *literal* is data inserted in a program. Numeric literals, 0.0585, 3.1416, 1024, for instance, may be placed in storage by a programmer and recalled whenever required for calculating. Alphabetic literals, such as TOTAL, GROSS PAY, THIS RECORD CONTAINS INVALID DATA, may also be stored and recalled when required.

Programs are composed of *routines,* or subdivisions, which are performed when required. A typical program tests input records for
various characteristics, and on the basis of the results of these tests
performs different routines. For example, if the answer to Test A is
yes, to Test B is no, and to Test C is yes, Routine 1 is performed. This
type of programming logic is often displayed in a decision table, as
seen in Fig. 8-9. When a routine is completed, the program is instructed to go to some other portion of the program. The instruction
to which a program goes to after completing a series of instructions is
marked with a *label,* an alphanumeric word identifying a location in a
program. When a program moves from one routine to another, it is
called a *branch.* Thus, when a main routine is being executed, and test
results dictate that a specific routine should be executed next, the
program branches to that routine, executes it, and branches then to
the label identifying the next instruction to be executed.

A *loop* is a routine that repeats itself as many times as instructed by
the program. For example, the equation to calculate the balance in a
savings account is (PRIN × RATE) + PRIN. This routine will calculate
the new balance for one year when compounding is done annually.
To calculate the new balance after a four-year period, a program
would loop through this routine four times.

Conditions				
Test A	Yes	Yes	No	No
Test B	No	Yes	Yes	No
Actions				
Perform Routine 1	✓	✓		
Perform Routine 2		✓	✓	
Perform Routine 3	✓	✓	✓	✓

Figure 8-9. A simple decision table.

STRUCTURED PROGRAMMING

Many business organizations today establish rigid standards for their
programming staff to follow when creating programs. A method
known as structured programming requires a modular approach; that

is, a general model of the program is first designed, and each component, or module, in that design is then fully developed. This programming style is often pictured as a tree, where the few large branches growing near the trunk eventually divide into smaller branches until the entire tree is filled out.

For the sake of simplicity and uniformity, programming patterns in structured programming are restricted to three formats: linear or serial, where one instruction follows another; selection, where one routine or another is chosen, depending upon the results of tests; and looping, where a routine is repeated a specific number of times.

Although structured programming is usually more difficult to learn than the traditional methods, it forces a programmer to think through his programming logic more thoroughly and leads to better organized, more uniform programs. Ultimately, the time spent to maintain these programs is greatly reduced, resulting in a cost saving to the organization.

MAKING IT PRACTICAL

The student council of your college has asked for your assistance in developing a computerized listing of the student body. Current plans call for having each student complete a data form during registration for the next semester and having this data keypunched and key verified at the college's data processing facilities. The student council is unclear as to what information it requires and expects you to design a form that will show the data that you recommend be recorded. Hardware constraints at the college limit you to 80-column card input.

1. Decide on what data you suggest recording.
2. Design the form for collecting this data.
3. If facilities are available, keypunch 10 sample records in the format you have designed.

REVIEW QUESTIONS

1. Distinguish between low-level and high-level languages.
2. List the steps required in program writing.
3. Distinguish between a compiler and an assembler.
4. What is meant by a "clean compile"?
5. What is included in programming documentation?

6. Describe what an ADD instruction looks like in machine language.

7. Name three functions of a compiler.

8. What types of errors can a compiler detect? What error types can they not detect?

9. Name two sources of data for a program.

10. In IBM/360 machine language, how many bytes of storage are required for an ADD instruction?

GLOSSARY

Assembler—a translator program that generates one machine language instruction for each symbolic instruction

Address—a locatable storage position

Branch—the movement of a program from one routine to another

Coding Sheet—a form for recording programming instructions

Compiler—a translator program that almost always generates more than one machine language instruction for each symbolic instruction

Debug—to correct errors in a program

Diagnostic Listing—a listing of grammatical and structural errors detected by a compiler

Label—an alphanumeric word identifying a location in a program

Loop—a routine that repeats itself within a program

Machine Language—a language with which a computer can work

Module—a portion of a program

Routine—a subdivision of a program

Operand—an address in storage where data being worked upon is stored

Operation Code—a command to the computer to carry out a particular step

Structured Programming—a programming method that imposes rigid standards in program construction

9

Programming Logic

Objectives

Programs for business applications follow definite patterns. Files must be updated, data summarized and selected, and reports printed.

Programmers use specific symbols to display various programming steps. These symbols are linked in a logical flow of ideas, called a flowchart.

This chapter examines the logical programming steps used to perform routine business applications and will demonstrate how to display these steps in a flowchart.

PROGRAMMING FLOWCHARTS

Programming logic is expressed in a programming flowchart, or block diagram. Programming flowcharts have two functions: they assist the programmer in his thought process as he creates the program, and they provide documentation for his successors when programs must be modified.

The standard flowcharting template, illustrated in Fig. 9-1, contains all the symbols required for flowcharting. For now, only the five symbols in Fig. 9-2 will be used.

Flowcharts are diagrams that depict the logical steps in a program. They consist of a series of symbols connected by flowlines. The symbols show the type of step being performed and what is taking place during these steps. The flowlines indicate which step follows which. A flowchart is essentially an outline of the steps that the programmer will use in a program. Figure 9-3 illustrates a flowchart for an elementary problem.

AN ELEMENTARY PROGRAM

Problem 1—A Card-to-Printer Problem

The student council of Harper Valley Junior College has compiled a punched card file consisting of one card for each student attending the college during the current semester. The record format is

Columns	Data	
1–20	Name (first name first)	
21–26	Date of birth (month, day, year)	
27	Sex (male = 1; female = 2)	
28–29	Year of graduation	
30–38	Social security number	
39	Sex appeal code	1 = beautiful or handsome
		2 = cute
		3 = OK
		4 = unappealing
40	Marital status	1 = single
		2 = married
		3 = divorced or separated
		4 = widowed

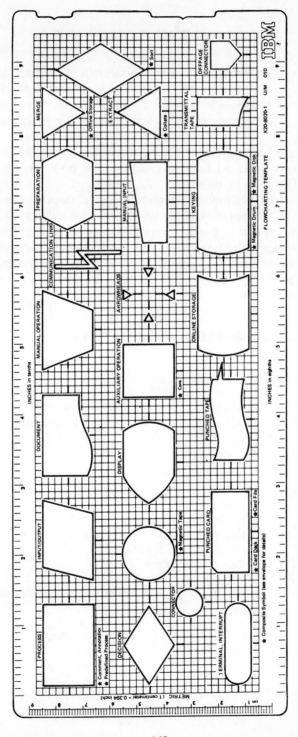

Figure 9-1. A template containing the symbols for programming.

168

Symbol	Name	Typical Use
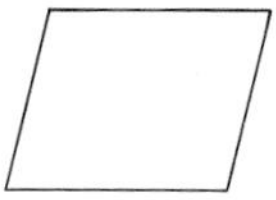 *(parallelogram)*	Input/Output	reading files; writing records
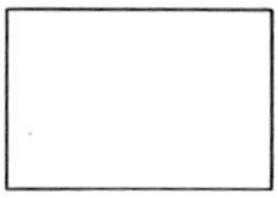 *(rectangle)*	Process	adding, subtracting, multiplying, dividing, moving data
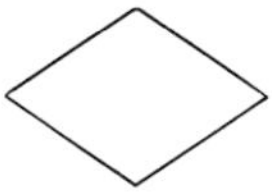 *(diamond)*	Decision	comparing two quantities; checking for end of file
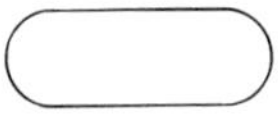 *(terminal shape)*	Terminal	beginning the run; stopping the run
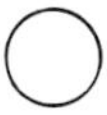 *(circle)*	Connector	continuing the program

Figure 9-2.   Basic symbols used for flowcharting.

List the file on a printer, using one line for each record. Figure 9-4 shows the input and output for this problem.

Solving the Problem

This basic computer program requires reading data from a punched card file and writing it on a printer. To do this, the programmer must write instructions to direct the computer and its input/output devices. An input device, in this case a card reader, sends data, one record at a time, to an area of the central processor that has been designated as the read-in area by the programmer. Instructions direct the computer to copy that information into a predetermined write-out area. When a write command is given, the entire content of the write-out area is transmitted to the printer, where one line of print is produced. The cycle—read a record, copy its content into a write-out area, and write that data on the printer—is repeated until the entire file has been processed (Fig. 9-5).

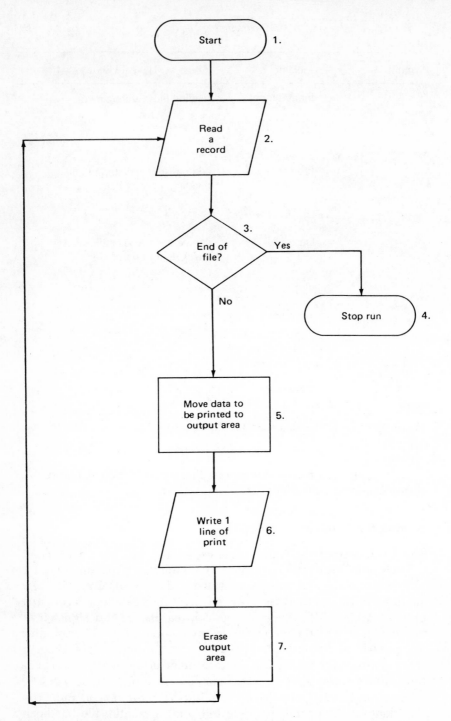

Figure 9-3. Flowchart for a card-to-printer program.

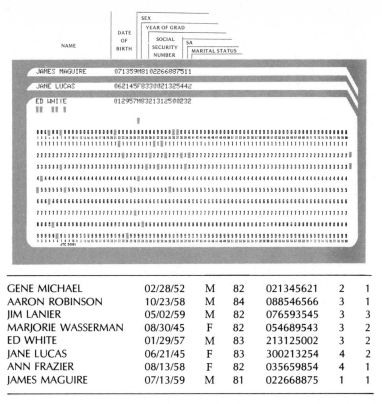

GENE MICHAEL	02/28/52	M	82	021345621	2	1
AARON ROBINSON	10/23/58	M	84	088546566	3	1
JIM LANIER	05/02/59	M	82	076593545	3	3
MARJORIE WASSERMAN	08/30/45	F	82	054689543	3	2
ED WHITE	01/29/57	M	83	213125002	3	2
JANE LUCAS	06/21/45	F	83	300213254	4	2
ANN FRAZIER	08/13/58	F	82	035659854	4	1
JAMES MAGUIRE	07/13/59	M	81	022668875	1	1

Figure 9-4. (a) Sample input cards for the card-to-printer listing. (b) Print-out from the card-to-printer listing.

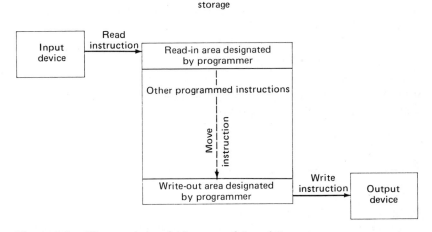

Figure 9-5. The computer during a card-to-printer program.

171

Figure 9-3 contains the detailed steps required to solve this problem. Analyze each step with the explanation below. Notice which symbols are used for each type of instruction.

Steps	Explanation
1.	The terminal symbol is used to indicate the beginning of the program.
2.	The input/output symbol is used to read one logical record. In processing punched card files, the instruction corresponding to this symbol causes the computer to physically read one card from the card reader and transfer its data to primary storage.
3.	This decision step asks whether an end-of-file indicator has been detected. In IBM computers, end of file for punched card files is indicated by a card with a slash (/) in column one and an asterisk (*) in column two. The end of a tape file is signaled by a special magnetic spot located after the last record on the tape.
4.	This program is terminated when the end-of-file indicator is detected.
5.	The programmer establishes areas for storing input and output. When a read instruction is executed, data is transferred from an input device to the input area in main memory designated by the programmer. Write instructions take what is located in the write-out area and transfer it to an output device. Step 5 in the flowchart copies the data stored by the read instruction into the write-out area, from where it can be written.
6.	The contents of the write-out area are transferred to an output device and printed.
7.	Spaces are moved to the write-out area so that it will be clear when new data is put there.

The program then returns to the read instruction, forming a continuous loop. The program repeats this loop until the end-of-file indicator is detected and the run is stopped.

Important Concepts in the Program

Data is read from an input device into a read-in area established by the programmer. It is then transferred to a programmer-created write-out area from where it is printed. These steps continue until the entire file is processed.

SOME VARIATIONS OF THE CARD TO
PRINTER PROBLEM

Problem 2—A Card-to-Printer Problem Using Headings

List the students of Harper Valley Junior College as in problem 1, but include appropriate column headings at the top of each page. (See Fig. 9-6.)

NAME	DATE OF BIRTH	SEX	YR OF GRAD	SOC SEC NUM	SA CODE
LARRY MAHONEY	09/18/61	1	81	093241453	1
NANCY ENGLISH	09/14/60	2	80	043261865	1
EDNA BESSINGER	10/17/57	2	79	091561984	4
CHARLES KELLER	12/01/59	1	80	210541812	2
HARVEY TALL	10/28/58	1	79	083410756	1
MARY SMALL	11/30/48	2	78	181321492	2
LINDA LAFEMINA	01/07/54	2	78	110311066	1
O. LEO LEAHY	07/12/60	1	82	107421789	1
MARVIN DOGOOD	08/13/59	1	81	113302475	3

Figure 9-6.

Solving the Problem

Before writing the detailed instructions, the programmer defines the precise words that he wishes to use in a heading. These words are to be printed at the top margin of every page in the report. The programmer then instructs the computer how to detect the bottom margin of each page and how to skip to the top margin of each subsequent page before printing the heading (Fig. 9-7).

Steps	Explanation
1–7.	Same as previous program.
8.	After every line is printed and the write-out area cleared, the program checks to see whether the bottom margin of a page has been reached. This is done either by detecting an end-of-page indicator on the printer or by counting each line as it is printed and comparing the total to the number of lines known to fit on the size of paper being used. When the bottom line has not

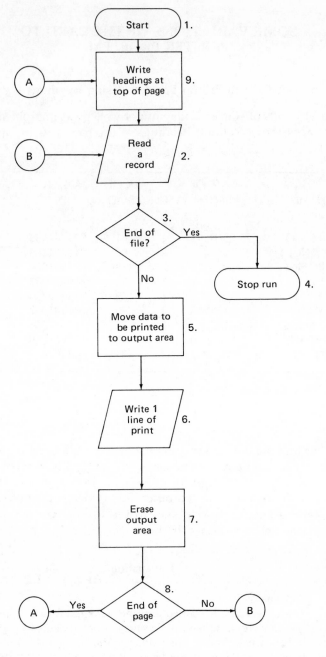

Figure 9-7. A flowchart for a card-to-printer listing with headings.

been reached, the program loops back to connector B and reads the next record. When end of page has been reached, the program returns to connector A, where headings will be printed.

9. The program directs the printer to skip to the top of each page and space down about one inch before printing. The words in the heading are then copied into the write-out area and written. Notice that step 9 is performed as the first step in the program so that the heading is printed at the top of the first page as well as the top of each following page.

Important Concepts in the Program

In programming business reports headings are usually printed at the top of each page. This is done for the first page by printing a heading even before the first card is read. It is done for subsequent pages by checking for the bottom margin on each page, and when it is detected, skipping to the top of the next page.

In initiating a program, a programmer stores alphabetical or numerical values within the central processor. This data may be used when required in the program.

Problem 3—Selecting Data

List all single females born in 1956 or later contained in the student master file of Harper Valley Junior College (Fig. 9-8).

LISTING OF SINGLE FEMALES
BORN IN 1956 OR LATER

NAME	DATE OF BIRTH
JANET ORRELL	05/25/56
NANCY ENGLISH	09/01/60
KIM WARREN	08/13/62

Figure 9-8. Output from selected listing.

Solving the Problem

Each record must be tested to see whether it has the prescribed characteristics. When a record does not meet the qualifications, it is rejected, and the next record is examined. Only records passing all tests are printed (Fig. 9-9).

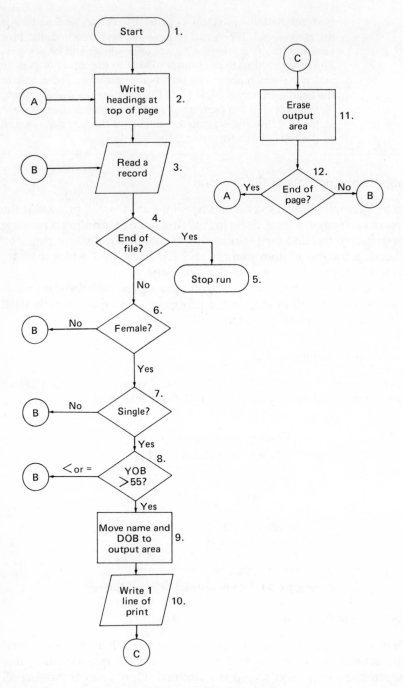

Figure 9-9.   A flowchart for listing selected records.

176

Steps	Explanation
1.	The beginning of the program.
2.	Headings are written at the top of the first page and every subsequent page.
3.	The student file is read into main memory one record at a time.
4–5.	When end of file is detected, the run is stopped.
6.	Sex code in each record is examined to see whether the student is male or female. If the record does not represent a female, the program ignores it by reading another record.
7.	Marital status of all females is examined. Any record not coded as single is rejected by reading another record.
8.	Year of birth is compared with 55. If year of birth is less than or equal to 55, the record is rejected.
9.	Only records representing single females born in 1956 or later get to step 9. All other records have been rejected. The name and date of birth for those selected are copied from the input area into the output area.
10.	Name and date of birth are printed on the same line.
11.	The output area is cleared.
12.	End of page is tested. When the bottom margin has been reached, the program returns to point A, where headings are written at the top of the next page. When page end is not reached, the next record is read.

Important Concepts in the Program

The program examines data, selects appropriate records, and rejects those that do not meet its specifications. This is done by comparing data to constants inserted in a program, or to other data. Generally, there are two types of comparisons: a simple comparison such as "Does A = B?" and high/low/equal comparisons like "Is A greater than, equal to, or less than B?"

OTHER BASIC PROBLEMS

Problem 4—Calculating Totals

Print the total of male students and the overall number of students at Harper Valley Junior College. (See Fig. 9-10.)

TOTAL STUDENTS	0028	TOTAL MALES	0016

Figure 9-10. Output from totals program.

Solving the Problem

The problem requires printing two totals: the number of males and the number of students in the school. As each record is read, one is added to a counter for totaling the number of students. If the record has a male code, one is also added to a different counter. These counters will contain the required totals when the end-of-file record is read, and they will be printed then. (See Fig. 9-11.)

Steps	Explanation
1.	Begin the program.
2.	The student file is read into main memory one record at a time.
3.	End of file initiates the end of job routine.
4.	If the record being examined is a data record and not an end-of-file indicator, one is added to a counter called "record-count." Record-count is a programmer-defined counter within main memory used for counting the total number of records being processed. Record-count will contain the number of records in the file when end of file is indicated.
5.	The record is tested for male code. If the code does not represent a male, the record is ignored and the next record is read.
6.	One is added to a counter called "male-count." This counter will contain the number of males in the school when end of file is indicated. The program then reads the next record.
7.	At end of file, the two totals, male-count and record-count, are copied from the counters to the output area.
8.	Totals are printed.
9.	The run is stopped.

Important Concepts in the Program

Arithmetic is performed in counters within the main memory of the computer. A programmer may set up as many counters as is required. One is added to a counter when each record is read, and one is added to a different counter for each male. Totals are printed when end of file is recognized.

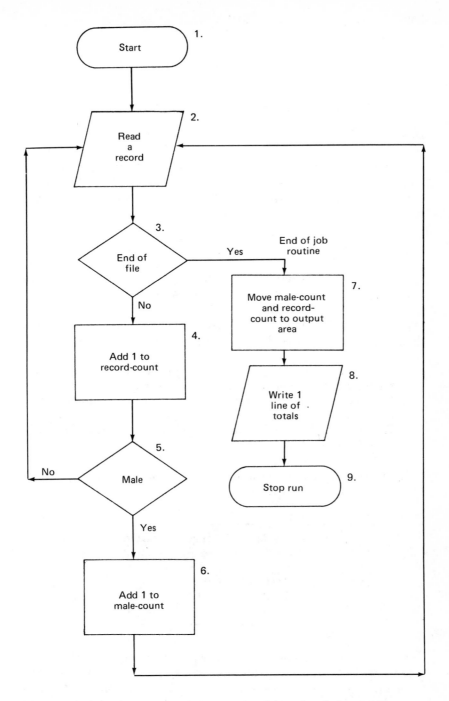

Figure 9-11.   A program that uses counters for accumulating totals.

SOLVING OTHER PROBLEMS

Problem 5—Using Routines; Solving Logical Problems

Determine the amount of FICA tax to be withheld from each employee on a company's payroll. FICA tax is the amount taken out of employees' pay for social security purposes. For this problem, assume that each employee contributes 6 percent of each weekly pay for the first $18,000 earned each year. The actual FICA rate and the base earnings on which it is taken vary from year to year.

Solving the Problem

Calculating FICA tax requires precise programming logic. Taxes are paid at a given rate each pay period until the individual has reached a certain year-to-date amount. (The rate is rounded to 6 percent and the taxable limit to 18,000 in this problem for ease in calculation.) Three distinct possibilities must be considered:

1. Employees whose year-to-date gross pay has already exceeded $18,000 and have thus paid the full FICA tax for the year.
2. Employees whose current earnings + year-to-date gross pay does not exceed $18,000.
3. Employees whose current earnings + year-to-date gross pay exceed $18,000 for the first time.

FICA tax is calculated by multiplying the taxable earnings by the FICA rate. Examine this table:

Name	Year-to-date Gross Pay	Current Earnings	Taxable Amount	FICA Tax
Dimaggio	19,000	600.00	-0-	-0-
Henrich	6,000	600.00	600.00	36.00
Keller	17,800	600.00	200.00	12.00

Although each employee earns $600.00 in the pay period, taxable amount varies because year-to-date gross pay varies. This is possible when one employee has been with a company for the entire year and others have joined at various times during the year. Dimaggio pays no FICA tax, because his year-to-date gross pay exceeds $18,000.

Henrich pays 6 percent of his entire weekly earnings, because his year-to-date gross pay + current earnings do not exceed $16,000. Of the $600.00 that Keller makes, $200.00 is subject to 6 percent tax, with the remaining $400.00 tax free. (See Fig. 9-12.)

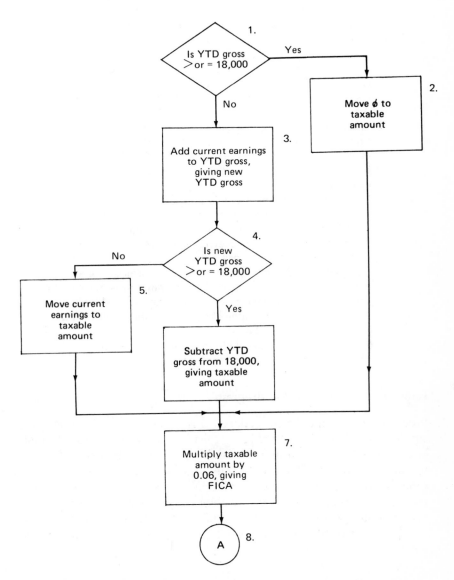

Figure 9-12.   The routine for calculating FICA tax in a payroll program.

Steps	Explanation
1.	This step is not the beginning of the program, but rather a continuation of the payroll program. Other sections, or routines, would calculate deductions other than FICA and determine an individual's gross and net pay. In Step 1, a person's year-to-date gross pay (the amount of money earned from January 1 until this current pay period) is compared with the maximum taxable figure for FICA.
2.	When year-to-date gross pay exceeds or equals $18,000, the employee has already paid the full FICA tax for the current year, and a 0 is placed in a storage location called Taxable-Amount.
3.	When year-to-date gross pay is less than $18,000, the new, or updated, year-to-date gross is calculated by adding current earnings to old year-to-date gross pay. Current earnings are contained in an input record or calculated elsewhere in the program.
4.	New year-to-date gross pay is compared with $18,000.
5.	When new year-to-date gross pay still does not equal or exceed $18,000, the entire current earnings are taxable.
6.	The only records that will reach Step 6 are for employees whose new year-to-date gross pay exceeds $18,000 for the first time this pay period. Some of their weekly earnings for this pay period is taxable; some is not. Taxable amount is calculated by subtracting the old year-to-date gross pay from $18,000.
7.	Taxable amount is multiplied by 0.06, and the result is stored in a storage area called FICA.
8.	The program continues with additional calculations.

Important Concepts in the Program

Programs are composed of sections, or routines, for completing specific tasks. In the routine for FICA calculation, taxable amount must be calculated for three different conditions. When the original year-to-date exceeds $18,000, the taxable amount is 0; when the original year-to-date + current earnings still does not equal or exceed $18,000, the entire current earnings are taxable; when the current earnings + year-to-date gross pay exceeds $18,000 for the first time in the current pay period, taxable earnings equal $18,000 less year-to-date gross pay.

Problem 6—Report Writing

Using the sales cards illustrated below, print a report of total sales per salesman and total sales for the company. The cards have been sorted into salesman's number order, and each card represents one sale.

The card layout is

Columns	Data
1–3	Salesman's number
4–7	Amount of sale

The report is shown in Fig. 9-13.

SALESMAN'S REPORT

SALESMAN'S NUMBER		AMOUNT OF SALE		
001		400		
001		300		
001		500		
	TOTAL FOR SALESMAN		001	1,200
004		600		
004		250		
004		125		
004		400		
	TOTAL FOR SALESMAN		004	1,375
007		200		
007		900		
	TOTAL FOR SALESMAN		007	1,100
047		1,200		
047		300		
047		900		
	TOTAL FOR SALESMAN		047	2,400
	TOTAL FOR COMPANY			6,075

Figure 9-13. Salesman's report output.

Solving the Problem

The key step in this report is to compare the salesman's number being read with the salesman's number in the previous record. If these two numbers are equal, the record being read is for the same salesman as the previous one. When the salesman's number being read is greater than the previous salesman's number, the first record for a different salesman has been detected and all work on the previous salesman must be completed. When the number being read is less than the previous number, a sequence error exists.

For this comparison, each salesman's number must be copied into an area of storage where it is saved. Allowance must also be made for the first record, because it has no previous record to be compared to.

A look at the report shows that a line of print results from each record read. This is known as a *detail line*. A total, known as a *minor total*, is printed after all the records for a salesman have been processed. Finally, the total sales for the company are printed at the end of each report. This is an overall, or final, total. (See Fig. 9-14.)

Step	Explanation
1.	Headings are written at the top of the first page.
2.	The first record is read.
3.	The end-of-file card initiates the end-of-job routine. Otherwise, the first record is processed as a normal record.
4.	The heading routine is performed at the top of every page except the first page.
5.	This is the normal read instruction. It reads every record except the first one.
6.	The end-of-file card initiates the end-of-job routine. When it is not end of job, the record is compared to the previous salesman's record. Note that the first record bypasses the compare step, while all other records go through it.
7.	Sales amount for each record is added to a minor counter, which accumulates total sales by salesman.
8.	Sales amount is also added to a final counter that accumulates total sales for the company.
9.	The detail line is set up in the output area by copying the data from the input area.
10.	A detail line is written.
11.	The output area is cleared.
12.	The salesman's number is saved so that it can be compared with the next record.

13.   The program tests for bottom of page. If it is page end, the program goes to point A and performs the heading routine. If not, it goes to point B and reads the next record.

14.   This key step compares the salesman's number being read to the previous salesman's number, which is being saved. When the current number is less than the previous one, the program goes to a sequence error routine. When the number being read is equal to the previous one, the record is for the same salesman and the normal routine is performed. When the current salesman's number is less than the number saved, the first record for another salesman has been read, and a minor routine is performed.

Steps 15 through 18 comprise the minor routine, the steps performed when the first card of another salesman has been read.

15.   Salesman's number and amount of sales for the salesman just completed are copied into the output area. Note that a salesman's total is printed when the first record of the next salesman has been read.

16.   Salesman's number and the amount of sales are printed.

17.   The output area is cleared.

18.   Salesman's counter is reset to 0 so that it can begin accumulating the sales for the next salesman. The program then goes to the normal routine to process the first record of the next salesman. When this record is read, the minor routine has been performed, but the record itself has not been processed.

Steps 19 through 21 comprise a sequence error routine.

19.   Salesman's number and amount of sale are copied into the output area for identifying purposes. A sentence such as, "This record caused a sequence error" is also moved into the output area. The sentence would have been put into storage when the program was being set up.

20.   The error message is printed.

21.   The output area is cleared. After every line of print, the program returns to the instruction that checks for end of page.

Steps 22 through 27 comprise the end-of-job routine.

22.   When the end-of-file card is detected, all the detail cards have been processed. The totals for the last salesman in the file have been accumulated but have not been printed, since the first card for a succeeding salesman has not been read. Thus, the last salesman's number and amount of sales are copied into the output area.

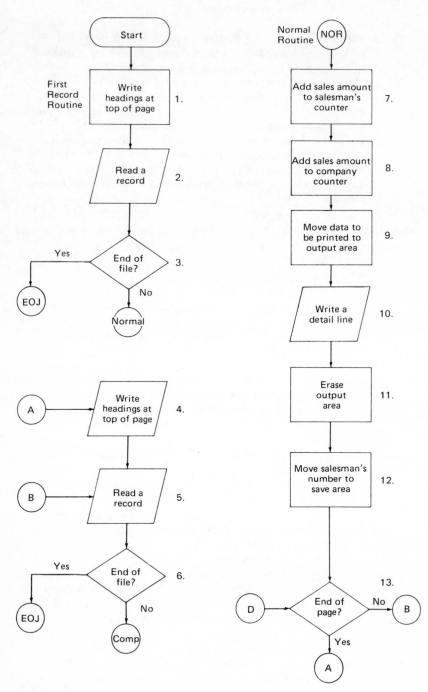

Figure 9-14. A flowchart for the salesman's report program.

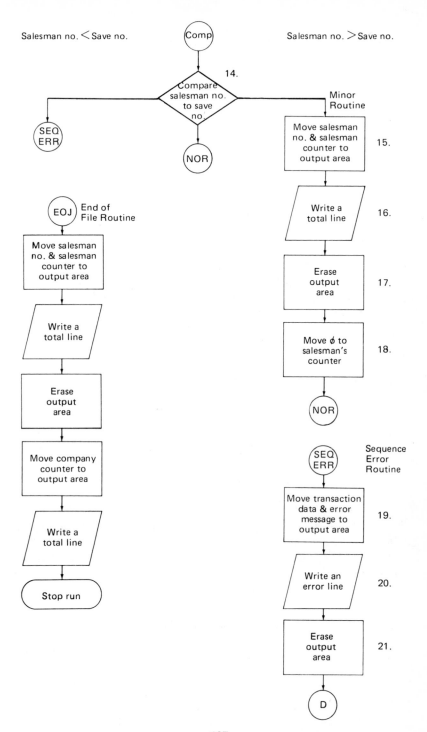

Salesman no. < Save no.

Comp

Salesman no. > Save no.

14.

Compare salesman no. to save no.

SEQ ERR

NOR

Minor Routine

Move salesman no. & salesman counter to output area — 15.

Write a total line — 16.

Erase output area — 17.

Move ∅ to salesman's counter — 18.

NOR

EOJ — End of File Routine

Move salesman no. & salesman counter to output area

Write a total line

Erase output area

Move company counter to output area

Write a total line

Stop run

SEQ ERR — Sequence Error Routine

Move transaction data & error message to output area — 19.

Write an error line — 20.

Erase output area — 21.

D

23.   The total for the last salesman is printed.
24.   The output area is cleared.
25.   The content of the counter accumulating the company's sales is
        moved into the output area.
26.   The company total is printed.
27.   The run is stopped.

MAKING IT PRACTICAL

The reports below are required by various administrators at Harper
Valley Junior College.

Flowchart a program to list all the single female students at Harper
Valley Junior College. Put an asterisk next to the names of those who were
born before January 1, 1958.

Sample listing:

Single Females Listing	
Name	**Born Before 1958**
Mary Backstage	*
Laura Ryan	
Frances Frye	*
Anne Rivers	

Flowchart the logic for a program to print the number of males,
females, and total graduates for each year of graduation. The input cards
have been sorted by social security number within each year of graduation.

Sample listing:

Students Statistical List			
Year	**Males**	**Females**	**Total**
80	1234	976	2210
81	1600	1423	3023
82	1555	1401	2956

The dean of the college requires a statistical analysis of the veterans in the class of 1981. The master file of punched cards is in social security number order. Data required is number of students, number of veterans, number of male veterans, number of female veterans, percentage of students who are veterans, percentage of students who are female veterans, and percentage of students who are male veterans.

Sample listing:

Class of 1981—Veteran Analysis

Total Students	Total Vets	Male Vets	Female Vets	% of Vet Students	% of Male Vets	% of Female Vets
3023	410	395	15	13.5%	13.0%	0.5%

REVIEW QUESTIONS

1. What functions do flowcharts perform?
2. Give examples of how each of the five basic symbols are used in flowcharting.
3. Explain how FICA tax is calculated.
4. Explain the use of read-in and write-out areas in programming.
5. How do programs detect the end of a file?
6. Why is the output area constantly cleared but the input area is not?
7. What is a high/low/equal compare?
8. Explain the use of headings. How does a program detect when to print them?
9. Explain how summary records are created and how they are used.

GLOSSARY

Arithmetic Constant—a numerical value inserted in a program

Block Diagram—a programming flowchart; a visual display of the logic in a program

Counter—a portion of main memory, set aside by the programmer, for accumulating totals

Detail Line—one line of print that corresponds to an input record

Error Message—a printed notification that the program has detected incorrect data

FICA—Federal Insurance Contributions Act; the tax deducted from employees for Social Security

Hard Copy—computer output, such as printed report, which can be read by a person

Heading—descriptive information at the top of a report

Loop—a programming technique in which the program returns to a specific instruction after completing a series of instructions

Minor Total—a total resulting from a change in controlling number of the least significant grouping

Overall Total—the final total printed at the end of a report

Programming Flowchart—a block diagram; a visual display of the logic in a program

Read-in Area—a programmer-defined portion of main memory that contains input data

Routine—a section or portion of a program

Summary Record—a data record, usually created as output from a computer program, that contains summarized data from a file

Write-out Area—a programmer-defined area of main memory that contains output data

Year-to-date Gross Pay—an individual's total earnings from January 1 until the beginning of the current pay period

10

Programming in COBOL

Objectives

In the previous chapter the logical steps for programming a problem's solution were examined. This chapter will demonstrate the requirements for the actual coding of simple computer programs and will serve as an introduction to COBOL, the most commonly used language for business applications. The student will learn the fundamental steps required to code a computer job and, if facilities are available, will be able to write an elementary program, debug it, and see it run correctly.

THE COBOL LANGUAGE

COBOL, *CO*mmon *B*usiness *O*riented *L*anguage, has been widely used in business programming since 1960. Devised by a joint committee of computer manufacturers, users, and representatives of the federal government, COBOL was created as a standard language for all computer manufacturers. Since its inception, COBOL has undergone many changes, and, in fact, several versions of COBOL exist today. The differences among these versions are technical and will not be discussed here.

COBOL is written with English words, making it comparatively easy to learn and to explain to a nonprogrammer. But it is written in a precise English form, with a specific vocabulary and exacting rules. The syntax of COBOL must be mastered before one qualifies as a professional programmer.

COBOL has several specific advantages as a programming language: it is machine-independent and can be used with the computers of all manufacturers; it facilitates the processing of business input and output files; it edits data easily, is standard throughout the industry, and, to a large extent, is self-documenting.

FORMAT FOR A COBOL PROGRAM

All COBOL programs have four divisions, which must appear in this order:

Identification Division	Gives the program a name and provides routine documentation.
Environment Division	Describes the computer that will compile the program and the computer upon which the job will be run. The Environment Division also assigns the files that will be used with the program to specific input/output devices.
Data Division	Describes the files that will be used with the program and the format of each of the records that the file contains in complete detail. The Data Division also defines other areas of storage that will be used by the program.
Procedure Division	Contains instructions for the computer to process data.

COBOL CODING SHEET

Figure 10-1 is a COBOL coding sheet containing a small portion of a program. Each line on the coding sheet results in one keypunched card. Note that programmers generally put a slash through zeroes to distinguish them from the letter O. The coding sheet contains these fields:

1–6	Sequence Number	This section permits the programmer to number each card in the program. The usual numbering system uses a page and line number for each card. The fifteenth card on the third coding sheet would be 003015.
7	Continuation or Comment	Column 7 serves two functions. First, column 7 contains a dash when a literal expression, such as words to be printed by the program or a number, must be continued from one line to another. An asterisk in column 7 allows the programmer to interject comments into his coding. These comments document the ideas contained in the program but are not actually instructions.
8	A Margin	Specific subdivisions of a COBOL program must begin at column 8 and may continue through column 72.
12	B Margin	Most statements in COBOL begin in column 12 and may continue through column 72.
73–80	Identification	Characters distinguishing one program from another may be placed here.

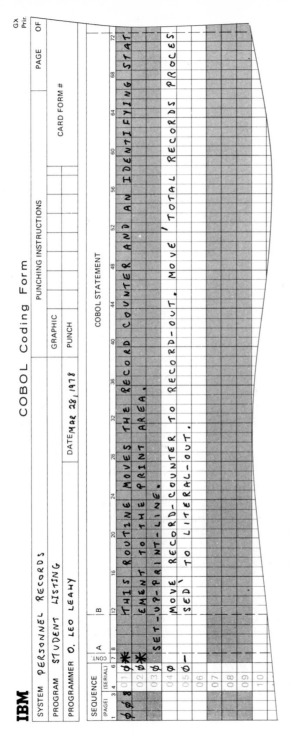

Figure 10-1. A COBOL coding of a program.

195

WRITING A COBOL PROGRAM

Identification Division

The first and easiest division to code is the Identification Division. The only entry required is PROGRAM-ID, which gives the program its name. Other entries are optional and may be used to provide documentation about the program. Study the sample Identification Division in Fig. 10-2, noting the punctuation, spacing, and the use of the A margin for each entry.

Environment Division

The Environment Division describes the hardware that will be used with the program. It contains two sections; the configuration section, which defines the computers with which the program will be compiled and run, and the input-output section, which assigns the files used with the program to specific hardware devices. The Environment Division, therefore, changes with each installation, so be sure to check for precise hardware descriptions wherever you are writing a program. The example in Fig. 10-3 is for an IBM System/370.

The source-computer is the CPU on which the program will be compiled; the object-computer is the CPU on which the job will be run. SYSIPT and SYSLST are symbolic names for a card reader and a printer at this particular installation. The names CARDIN and LIST are given by the programmer to the two files involved in the program: one an input deck of punched cards; the other, a printed listing of these cards.

Data Division

Examine the Data Division illustrated in Figs. 10-4 and 10-5. The two illustrations comprise one Data Division. Figure 10-4 describes a simple input file. The file is on punched cards and contains social security number in columns 1–9, name in 10–25, and date of birth in 26–31. Figure 10-5 shows the Data Division entries for printing these cards.

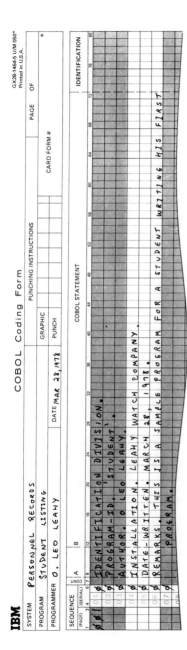

Figure 10-2. A COBOL identification division.

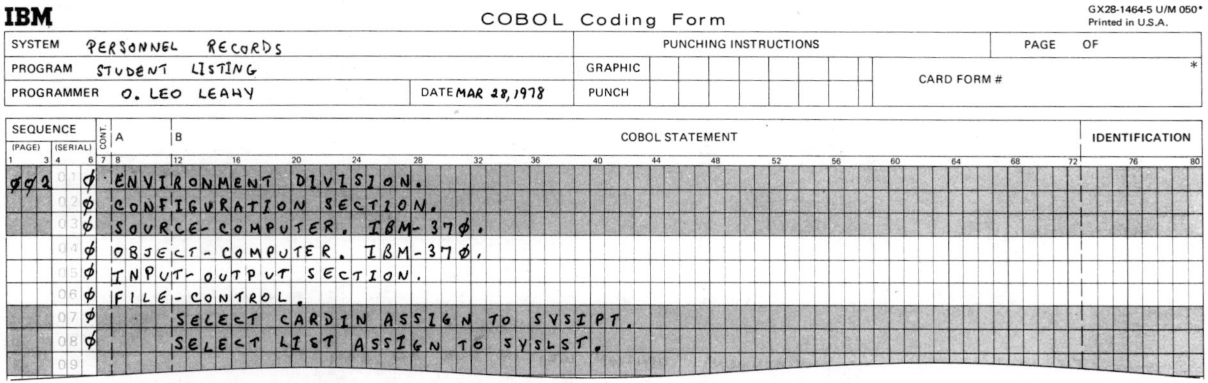

Figure 10-3. A COBOL environment division.

197

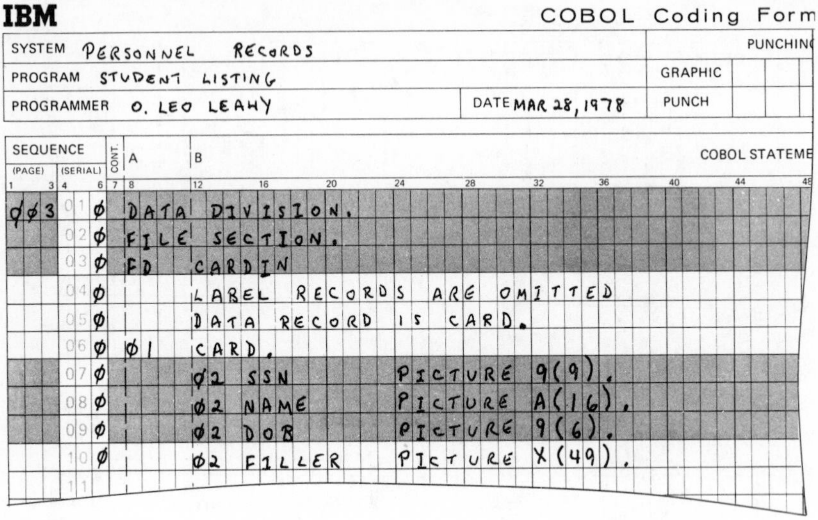

IBM   COBOL Coding Form

SYSTEM	PERSONNEL RECORDS		PUNCHING
PROGRAM	STUDENT LISTING	GRAPHIC	
PROGRAMMER	O. LEO LEAHY	DATE MAR 28, 1978	PUNCH

```
SEQUENCE       A   B                                    COBOL STATEME
(PAGE)(SERIAL)
ØØ3 01 Ø   DATA DIVISION.
    02 Ø   FILE SECTION.
    03 Ø   FD CARDIN
    04 Ø      LABEL RECORDS ARE OMITTED
    05 Ø      DATA RECORD IS CARD.
    06 Ø  Ø1  CARD.
    07 Ø      Ø2 SSN      PICTURE 9(9).
    08 Ø      Ø2 NAME     PICTURE A(16).
    09 Ø      Ø2 DOB      PICTURE 9(6).
    10 Ø      Ø2 FILLER   PICTURE X(49).
    11
```

Figure 10-4. Data division describing an input card format.

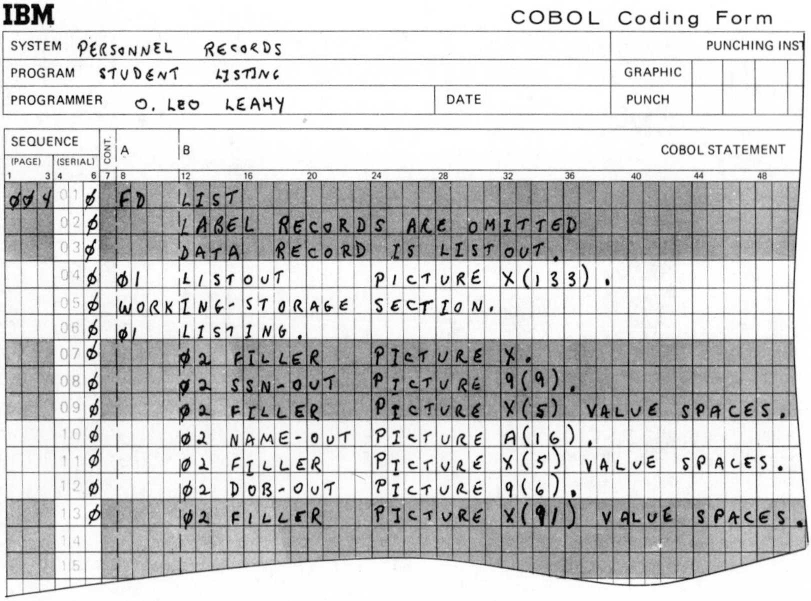

IBM   COBOL Coding Form

SYSTEM	PERSONNEL RECORDS		PUNCHING INST
PROGRAM	STUDENT LISTING	GRAPHIC	
PROGRAMMER	O. LEO LEAHY	DATE	PUNCH

```
SEQUENCE       A   B                                    COBOL STATEMENT
(PAGE)(SERIAL)
ØØ4 01 Ø   FD LIST
    02 Ø      LABEL RECORDS ARE OMITTED
    03 Ø      DATA RECORD IS LISTOUT.
    04 Ø  Ø1  LISTOUT      PICTURE X(133).
    05 Ø   WORKING-STORAGE SECTION.
    06 Ø  Ø1  LISTING.
    07 Ø      Ø2 FILLER    PICTURE X.
    08 Ø      Ø2 SSN-OUT   PICTURE 9(9).
    09 Ø      Ø2 FILLER    PICTURE X(5) VALUE SPACES.
    10 Ø      Ø2 NAME-OUT  PICTURE A(16).
    11 Ø      Ø2 FILLER    PICTURE X(5) VALUE SPACES.
    12 Ø      Ø2 DOB-OUT   PICTURE 9(6).
    13 Ø      Ø2 FILLER    PICTURE X(91) VALUE SPACES.
    14
    15
```

Figure 10-5. Data division describing printer output.

Although the Data Division seems complex at first view, an analysis of its entries shows that it contains a logical description of the data being processed. Figure 10-4 illustrates:

File Description and Record Description. The input file is described with the level number FD (hexadecimal) starting in column 8. Since the file being described is an 80-column punched card input file, the entries are relatively easy. The file is given a name CARDIN, the same name that was assigned to the card reader in the INPUT-OUTPUT section of the Environment Division. The phrase LABEL RECORDS ARE OMITTED refers to writing output labels identifying reels of tape. Since there are no labels on punched cards, the labels are omitted. RECORDING MODE IS F tells the computer that the length of each input record is fixed (F) at 80 columns. DATA RECORD IS CARD names the detail record in the file.

The record description begins with the number 01 at the A margin. Recall that a record is a group of related fields and a file is a group of related records. The record description describes the format of each record in the file. Since the record in the problem is an 80-column card, all 80 columns must be described. Each field in the record will require one line on the coding sheet. Each line contains:

- *level numbers.* Each field's description begins with the level number 02 in the B margin. 02 is used because it represents a subdivision of 01. If a field were subdivided, such as DOB (date of birth) divided into month, day, and year, a number greater than 02 would be used to identify these subfields.
- *data names.* Each field is given a programmer-supplied name. Any name may be used, provided that there are no spaces in the name, that it contains at least one alphabetic character, and that it does not begin with a hyphen. Data names SSN, NAME, and DOB are made up by the programmer and are not COBOL language words. FILLER is a COBOL reserved word used to describe fields that are blank.
- *data pictures.* The characteristics of each field are described with a symbolic picture. The word PICTURE is literally spelled out, and the field description follows. Data is either alphabetic, numeric, or mixed (alphanumeric). Alphabetic data is described with the letter A, numeric with the number 9, and alphanumeric with the letter X. SSN, the field for social security number, contains 9 numeric characters, NAME contains 16 alphabetic characters, and DOB contains 6 numeric characters. Since all punched card records have 80 characters, the record description must be filled out with 49 blank spaces using the COBOL word FILLER.

Figure 10-5 shows the Data Division entries for a listing on a printer. They are similar to the input descriptions, with these exceptions:

- The FD entry now describes LIST, the name assigned to the printer in the INPUT-OUTPUT section of the Environment Division.
- The coding contains two record descriptions, LISTOUT and LISTING. LISTOUT represents an all-purpose output area to which data must be moved before it is printed. LISTING, which describes the print line used in this program, is a record in the working-storage section of the Data Division. Working-storage is used to contain the results of data being worked upon or data that will be printed. For example, counters for accumulating totals and headings are contained in working-storage. When data is to be printed, it is moved from working-storage to the all-purpose output area and written.
- The record description LISTING describes the 133 print positions used on this model of printer. The first print position that contains a FILLER is reserved for spacing and skipping control for the high-speed printer.
- Each field is given a unique data name supplied by the programmer. Between each field is a 5-position FILLER to space the output neatly horizontally across the page. The final FILLER provides spaces to total 133, the number of spaces available on the printer (Fig. 10-6).

Procedure Division

The Procedure Division consists of instructions for the computer to execute. The flowcharts of the previous chapter were actually outlines of procedure divisions. The Procedure Division shows some of the advantages of COBOL; for instance, sentences are written in English using COBOL reserved words and programmer-provided data names and paragraph markers.

The basic COBOL vocabulary of reserved words is contained in Fig. 10-7. Most of these words have technical uses beyond the level that COBOL is being studied here.

COBOL coding generally follows the rules of English grammar. Sentences end with periods, commas may be inserted when clarification is desired, words must have spaces between them, and periods are followed by spaces. Programmer-defined data names are limited to 31 characters and must not contain spaces, which is why so many hyphenated words such as GROSS-PAY and YEAR-TO-DATE-PAY appear in programs. Instructions are generally written in paragraph form, but sometimes beginners prefer to write one sentence per line on a coding sheet.

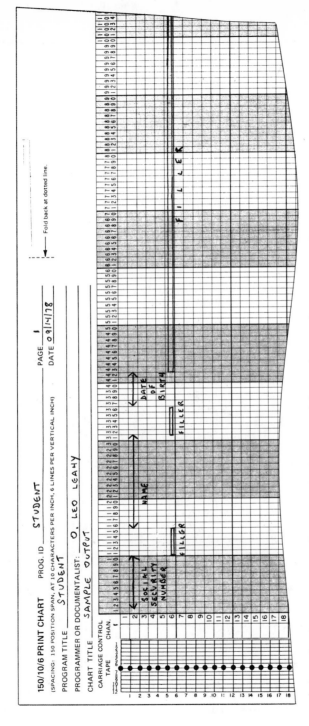

Figure 10-6. A printer spacing chart for listing social security number, name, and date of birth.

ACCEPT	DATE-WRITTEN	INDICATE
ACCESS	DE	INITIATE
ACTUAL	DECIMAL-POINT	INPUT
ADD	DECLARATIVES	INPUT-OUTPUT
ADDRESS	DEPENDING	INSTALLATION
ADVANCING	DESCENDING	INTO
AFTER	DETAIL	INVALID
ALL	DISPLAY	IS
ALPHABETIC	DIVIDE	JUST
ALTER	DIVISION	JUSTIFIED
ALTERNATE	DOWN	KEY
AND	ELSE	KEYS
ARE	END	LABEL
AREA	ENDING	LAST
AREAS	ENTER	LEADING
ASCENDING	ENVIRONMENT	LEFT
ASSIGN	EQUAL	LESS
AT	ERROR	LIMIT
AUTHOR	EVERY EXAMINE	LIMITS
BEFORE	EXIT	LINE
BEGINNING	FD	LINE-COUNTER
BLANK	FILE	LINES
BLOCK	FILE-CONTROL	LOCK
BY	FILE-LIMIT	LOW-VALUE
CF	FILE-LIMITS	LOW-VALUES
CH	FILLER	MEMORY
CHARACTERS	FINAL	
CLOCK-UNITS	FIRST	MODE
CLOSE	FOOTING	MODULES
COBOL	FOR	MOVE
CODE	FROM	MULTIPLE
COLUMN	GENERATE	MULTIPLY
COMMA	GIVING	NEGATIVE
COMP	GO	NEXT
COMPUTATIONAL	GREATER	NO
COMPUTE	GROUP	NOT
CONFIGURATION	HEADING	NOTE
CONTAINS	HIGH-VALUE	NUMBER
CONTROL	HIGH-VALUES	NUMERIC
CONTROLS	I-O	OBJECT-COMPUTER
COPY	I-O-CONTROL	OCCURS
CORR	IDENTIFICATION	OF
CORRESPONDING	IF	OFF
CURRENCY	IN	OMITTED
DATA	INDEX	ON
DATE-COMPILED	INDEXED	OPEN

Figure 10-7.   COBOL reserved words.

OPTIONAL	RERUN	SUBTRACT
OR	RESERVE	SUM
OUTPUT	RESET	SYNC
PAGE	RETURN	SYNCHRONIZED
PAGE-COUNTER	REVERSED	TALLY
PERFORM	REWIND	TALLYING
PF	RF	TAPE
PH	RH	TERMINATE
PIC	RIGHT	THAN
PICTURE	ROUNDED	THROUGH
PLUS	RUN	THRU
POSITION	SAME	TIMES
POSITIVE	SD	TO
PROCEDURE	SEARCH	TYPE
PROCEED	SECTION	UNIT
PROCESSING	SECURITY	UNTIL
PROGRAM-ID	SEEK	UP
QUOTE	SEGMENT-LIMIT	UPON
QUOTES	SELECT	USAGE
RANDOM	SENTENCE	USE
RD	SEQUENTIAL	USING
READ	SET	VALUE
RECORD	SIGN	VALUES
RECORDS	SIZE	VARYING
REDEFINES	SORT	WHEN
REEL	SOURCE	WITH
RELEASE	SOURCE-COMPUTER	WORDS
REMARKS	SPACE	WORKING-STORAGE
RENAMES	SPACES	WRITE
REPLACING	SPECIAL-NAMES	ZERO
REPORT	STANDARD	ZEROES
REPORTING	STATUS	ZEROS
REPORTS	STOP	

Figure 10-7. *(Cont.)*

Using COBOL verbs is the key to understanding the language. The COBOL verbs used in this Procedure Division and their meanings are:

OPEN	allows the CPU access to a file
CLOSE	disconnects a file from the CPU
READ	reads a record from an input device
WRITE	writes a record upon an output device
ADD	
SUBTRACT	perform arithmetic functions
MULTIPLY	
DIVIDE	
MOVE	copies data from one area in storage into another
GO TO	shifts the execution of programming instructions to a paragraph marker
STOP	informs the operating system that the program has been completed

These symbols may also be used in the Procedure Division.

=	equal
>	greater than
<	less than

Read the Procedure Division in Fig. 10-8. The instructions read each record from the input file CARDIN and write them in the format of the output record LISTING described in the Data Division. When the last record has been processed, the run stops. The illustration uses one line for each sentence in the Procedure Division and not the more standard format of paragraph construction.

The instructions in Fig. 10-8 also illustrate these points:

Paragraph Markers. START, A, and ENDJOB are paragraph markers pointing out specific areas of the program which may be referred to by the programmer.

COBOL Verbs. This elementary program uses seven COBOL verbs. Each is used as follows:

OPEN	the two files in the problem, CARDIN and LIST, are made available to the central processor.

IBM   COBOL Coding Form

SYSTEM		PUNCHING
PROGRAM	GRAPHIC	
PROGRAMMER	DATE	PUNCH

```
SEQUENCE    C
(PAGE)(SERIAL) O  A    B                              COBOL STATEME
1    3 4   6 7 8    12      16     20     24     28    32     36    40     44
ØØ5 01 Ø  PROCEDURE  DIVISION.
   02 Ø  START.
   03 Ø      OPEN INPUT CARDIN OUTPUT LIST.
   04 Ø  A.
   05 Ø      READ CARDIN AT END GO TO ENDJOB.
   06 Ø      MOVE SSN TO SSN-OUT.
   07 Ø      MOVE NAME TO NAME-OUT.
   08 Ø      MOVE DOB TO DOB-OUT.
   09 Ø      WRITE LISTOUT FROM LISTING AFTER 2.
   10 Ø      MOVE SPACES TO LISTOUT.
   11 Ø      GO TO A.
   12 Ø  ENDJOB.
   13 Ø      CLOSE CARDIN LIST
   14 Ø      STOP RUN.
   15
   16
   17
```

Figure 10-8. Procedure division for card-to-printer-program.

READ	Each record from the file CARDIN is read, one record at a time. The term AT END in the sentence refers to the time when the last record in the file has been processed, at which point the sequence of instructions skips to the paragraph marker ENDJOB.
MOVE	The move verb is used to copy the three items of data, SSN, NAME, and DOB from the input area to the output area. It also erases the output area by moving a string of spaces there.
GO TO	When the last record has been processed, the first GO TO transfers the sequence of instructions to ENDJOB. The second GO TO completes the basic loop in the program by continually returning to paragraph marker A to read the next record.
WRITE	This instruction writes one line for each record read.
CLOSE	The two files are disconnected from the CPU.
STOP	The CPU is informed that the run has been completed.

The entire program and its output listing are shown in Figs. 10-10 and 10-11.

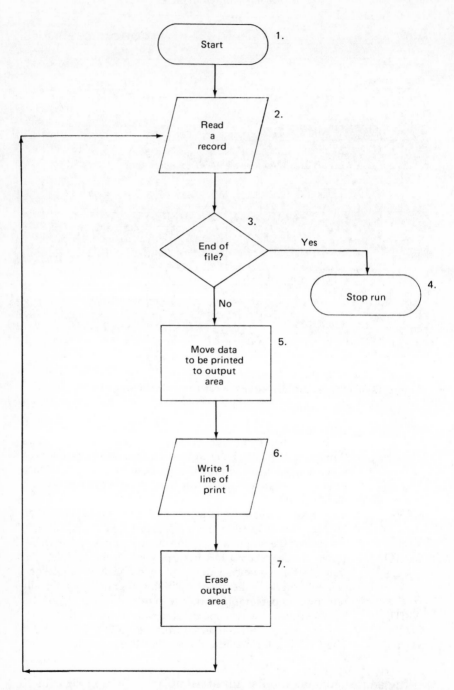

Figure 10-9. A flowchart for the procedure division in Figure 10-8.

321542108	ROY WHITE	032047
123654789	MICKEY RIVERS	021350
852356654	THURMON MUNSON	112149
654328742	ELMER VALO	052154
122353285	FRANK CROSETTI	053058
022168546	OSCAR GRIMES	052347
313853244	PETER SUDER	102359
022546327	JOHN MIZE	061154
221449352	EDGAR BAIRD	022360
188523462	GERALD DOHERTY	122561
311543208	JUSTINO ROSATI	052351
087653851	MARGE MARTIN	091959
321128546	MARY MAGOON	040555
032020232	NICK ETTEN	062443
120346852	DENTON YOUNG	072659

Figure 10-10. Sample output listing of social security number, name, and date of birth.

COBOL COMPILATION   STUDENT   SOURCE LISTING

1   IDENTIFICATION DIVISION.
2   PROGRAM-ID. 'STUDENT'.
3   AUTHOR. O LEO LEAHY.
4   INSTALLATION. LEAHY WATCH COMPANY.
5   DATE-WRITTEN. MARCH 21, 1978.
6   REMARKS. THIS IS A SAMPLE FOR A STUDENT WRITING HIS FIRST PROGRAM.
7   ENVIRONMENT DIVISION.
8   CONFIGURATION SECTION.
9   SOURCE-COMPUTER. IBM-370.
10 OBJECT-COMPUTER. IBM-370.
11 INPUT-OUTPUT SECTION.
12 FILE-CONTROL.
13   SELECT CARDIN ASSIGN TO SYSIPT.
14   SELECT LIST ASSIGN TO SYSLST.
15 DATA DIVISION.
16 FILE SECTION.
17 FD CARDIN
18   LABEL RECORDS ARE OMITTED
19   RECORDING MODE IS F
20   DATA RECORD IS CARD.
21 01 CARD.
22   02 SSN   PICTURE 9(9).
23   02 NAME   PICTURE A(16).
24   02 DOB   PICTURE 9(6).
25   02 FILLER   PICTURE X(49).

```
26   FD LIST
27         LABEL RECORDS ARE OMITTED
28         DATA RECORD IS LISTOUT.
29   01 LISTOUT          PICTURE X(133).
30   WORKING-STORAGE SECTION.
31   01 LISTING.
32         02 FILLER          PICTURE X.
33         02 SSN-OUT         PICTURE 9(9).
34         02 FILLER          PICTURE X(5) VALUE SPACES.
35         02 NAME-OUT        PICTURE A(16).
36         02 FILLER          PICTURE X(5) VALUE SPACES.
37         02 DOB-OUT         PICTURE 9(6).
38         02 FILLER          PICTURE X(91) VALUE SPACES.
39   PROCEDURE DIVISION.
40   START.
41         OPEN INPUT CARDIN OUTPUT LIST.
42   A.
43         READ CARDIN AT END GO TO ENDJOB.
44         MOVE SSN TO SSN-OUT.
45         MOVE NAME TO NAME-OUT.
46         MOVE DOB TO DOB-OUT.
47         WRITE LISTOUT FROM LISTING AFTER 2.
48         MOVE SPACES TO LISTOUT.
49         GO TO A.
50   ENDJOB.
51         CLOSE CARDIN LIST.
52         STOP RUN.
```

Figure 10-11. A listing of the program illustrated in the chapter.

209

CODING ANOTHER PROBLEM

Figure 10-12 illustrates records from an input statistical file for the students at Harper Valley Junior College. A program to count the number of students and the number of males contained in the file is required. Read the programmed solution contained in Fig. 10-13. Notice these differences from the previous program:

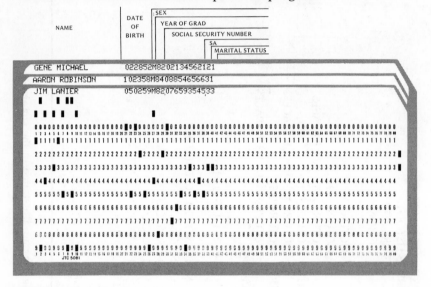

Figure 10-12.   Sample input to statistical program.

Environment Division

The Environment Division for this program is written for a UNIVAC 70 Model 45 computer.

Data Division

Since the input record is different from the previous program, the record description must change to describe the new card layout. One significant difference is that date of birth is divided into month, day, and year fields. Level number 03 indicates that each subfield is a component of field level 02.

The program requires two totals, one for a record count and one for number of males. A counter is set up for each of these with a 77 level entry in the working-storage section of the Data Division. The number 77 is a special level number for establishing work areas that are not part of other records. Each counter contains four positions and has an initial value of 0.

We have seen level numbers used for four different purposes:

- FD, a hexadecimal number, represents the file level.
- 01 represents the record level.
- 02 and 03 represent field levels, with 03 being a subdivision of 02.
- 77 represents an area independent of other data.

Working-storage also contains the layout for the one line of print required in the program. The output record, called TOTAL-LINE by the programmer, contains two fields, COUNT-OUT and MALE-OUT, which will receive the accumulated totals after the last record has been processed. TOTAL-LINE also contains alphabetic literals, TOTAL STUDENTS and TOTAL MALES, for identifying the output results.

Procedure Division

The Procedure Division in Fig. 10-13 illustrates these points (see also Figs. 10-14 and 10-15):

- Testing conditions in COBOL is done with IF statements. When IF statement conditions are met, the programmer includes a command to instruct the program what to do. In the example, when sex is not equal to 1, the program goes to A. When the test is not met, the program goes to the next sequential instruction. Thus, when sex is equal to 1, a 1 is added to MALE-COUNT. To count the number of records, the program adds 1 to the counter RECORD-COUNT as each record is read. When end of file is detected, RECORD-COUNT contains the number of records in the file.
- The WRITE instruction prints the contents of the record LISTOUT after the last record has been processed. Data to be printed is accumulated in the working-storage record TOTAL-LINE. The contents of RECORD-COUNT and MALE-COUNT are moved to appropriate fields in TOTAL-LINE. The instruction WRITE LISTOUT FROM TOTAL-LINE copies the entire TOTAL-LINE into LISTOUT and then prints it.

The two problems illustrate only the very basics of COBOL coding. The language is far more complex, because it must handle the complexities of the modern business community.

```
 1    IDENTIFICATION DIVISION.
 2    PROGRAM-ID. 'WCCC'.
 3    AUTHOR. O LEO LEAHY.
 4    ENVIRONMENT DIVISION.
 5    CONFIGURATION SECTION.
 6    SOURCE-COMPUTER. UNIVAC-70-45F.
 7    OBJECT-COMPUTER. UNIVAC-70-45F.
 8    INPUT-OUTPUT SECTION.
 9    FILE-CONTROL.
10        SELECT CARDIN ASSIGN TO SYSIPT.
11        SELECT LIST ASSIGN TO SYSLST.
12    DATA DIVISION.
13    FILE SECTION.
14    FD CARDIN
15        LABEL RECORDS ARE OMITTED
16        RECORDING MODE IS F
17        DATA RECORD IS CARD.
18    01 CARD.
19        02    NAME            PICTURE A(20).
20        02    DOB.
21        03    MONTH           PICTURE 99.
22              03 DAY          PICTURE 99.
23              03 YEAR         PICTURE 99.
24        02    SEX             PICTURE 9.
25        02    YRGRAD          PICTURE 99.
26        02    SOC-SEC         PICTURE 9(9).
27        02    SA              PICTURE 9.
28        02    FILLER          PICTURE X(41).
29    FD LIST
30        LABEL RECORDS ARE OMITTED
31        DATA RECORD IS LISTOUT.
32        01    LISTOUT         PICTURE X(133).
33    WORKING-STORAGE SECTION.
34    77        RECORD-COUNT    PICTURE 9(4) VALUE 0.
35    77        MALE-COUNT      PICTURE 9(4) VALUE 0.
36    01        TOTAL-LINE.
37        02    FILLER          PICTURE X.
38        02    FILLER          PICTURE X(14).    VALUE 'TOTAL STUDENTS'.
39        02    FILLER          PICTURE X(3)      VALUE SPACES.
40        02    COUNT-OUT       PICTURE 9(4).
41        02    FILLER          PICTURE X(15)     VALUE SPACES.
42        02    FILLER          PICTURE X(11)     VALUE 'TOTAL MALES'.
43        02    FILLER          PICTURE X(3)      VALUE SPACES.
44        02    MALE-OUT        PICTURE 9(4).
45        02    FILLER          PICTURE X(78)     VALUE SPACES.
46    PROCEDURE DIVISION.
47    START.
48        OPEN INPUT CARDIN OUTPUT LIST.
49        WRITE LISTOUT AFTER ADVANCING 0.
50    A.
51        READ CARDIN AT END GO TO ENDJOB.
52        ADD 1 TO RECORD-COUNT.
53        IF SEX NOT = 1 GO TO A.
54        ADD 1 TO MALE-COUNT.
55        GO TO A.
56    ENDJOB.
57        MOVE RECORD-COUNT TO COUNT-OUT.
58        MOVE MALE-COUNT TO MALE-OUT.
59        WRITE LISTOUT FROM TOTAL-LINE AFTER 2.
60        CLOSE CARDIN LIST.
61        STOP RUN.
```

Figure 10-13.   A program to count the number of students and number of males at Harper Valley Junior College.

212

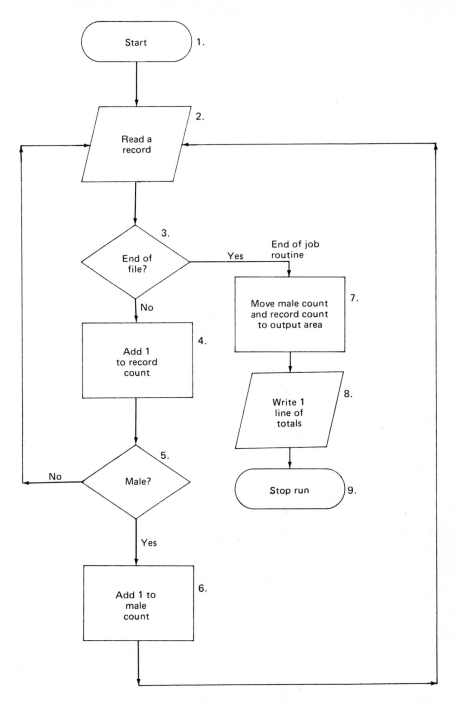

Figure 10-14. A flowchart for a program using counters.

213

TOTAL STUDENTS	0028	TOTAL MALES	0016

Figure 10-15. Output from statistical unit.

MAKING IT PRACTICAL

Code the portion of the file section of the data division that describes this input statistical file.

Columns	Data
1–20	Name
21–22	Occupation code
23–27	Annual salary (in whole dollars)
28–36	Social security number
37–42	Year of employment (month, day, year)
43–80	Blank

The company whose file is described above is about to give a 5 percent salary increase to each of its employees. Code a program that will print the name and new salary of each employee and count the number of employees in the organization. One of your fellow programmers has completed the data division for you and provided you with the flowchart opposite. He has labeled the output record LISTOUT and has WORKING-STORAGE records called DETAIL-LINE and TOTAL-LINE.

REVIEW QUESTIONS

1. How did COBOL originate?
2. Why is COBOL comparatively easy to learn?
3. Name the four divisions of a COBOL program.
4. Explain how punched cards in a program are usually numbered.
5. What functions do the Environment Division perform?
6. Differentiate between file descriptions and record descriptions.

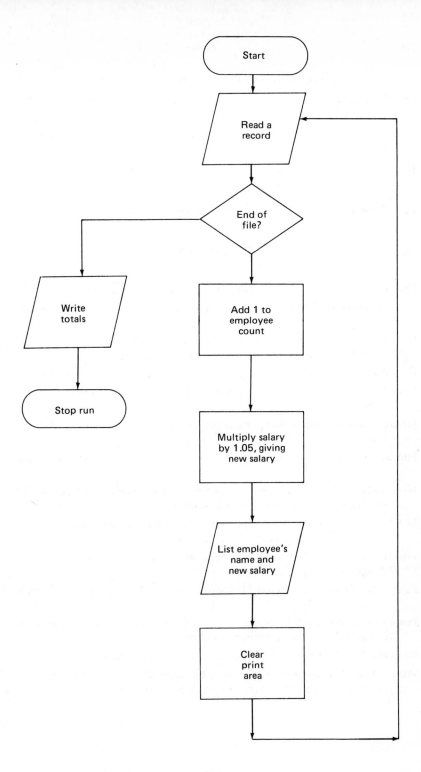

7. What are level numbers 01, FD, and 77 used for?

8. How is numeric, alphabetic, and alphanumeric data pictured in COBOL?

9. What is the relationship between the Procedure Division and a flowchart?

10. How are conditions tested in COBOL coding?

11. What does the WRITE instruction do?

12. Explain what a MOVE instruction does.

GLOSSARY

Coding Sheet—a form for recording programming instructions

Configuration Section—the portion of the Environment Division for describing the computers that will be used with the program

Data Division—that portion of a COBOL program that defines input and output files and records and other areas in storage

Data Name—a programmer-assigned word used in a COBOL program

Data Picture—a symbolic description of the data that a storage area will contain

Environment Division—that portion of a COBOL program that describes the hardware that will be used with the program

File Section—a portion of the Data Division for defining input and output data

Input-Output Section—a part of the Environment Division that assigns the files used with the program to specific I/O devices

Level Numbers—a numbering system used in the Data Division for identifying the relationship of one item of data with others

Literal—an alphabetic, numberic, or alphanumeric expression used in a program

Paragraph Marker—a term used to locate a series of instructions in a COBOL program

Procedure Division—that portion of a COBOL program that contains the commands for the computer to follow

Reserved Word—a word that is part of the basic COBOL vocabulary

Working-Storage Section—a portion of the Data Division for defining areas of storage where the program's work is to be done

IV

Applying the Computer to Business Problems

11

Computerized Accounts Receivable

Objectives

Basic accounting systems are performed in much the same way in most businesses. Each organization has its own peculiarities and business needs, but certain fundamental steps are always done.

Accounts receivable is the process of determining what is owed to a company and collecting that money. To do this, sales on account and cash receipts must be recorded and applied to individual customer's accounts. The customer must be apprised immediately of the amount of each sale on account through an invoice, and regularly of the outstanding balance in his account through a billing statement.

This chapter illustrates how these steps are typically done by computer.

PROCESSING RECEIVABLES MANUALLY

Accounts receivable is the process of determining customer balances. In its simplest form, it has three components:

1. The balance brought forward from a previous period.
2. Sales on account to customers, which increase the balance owed.
3. Cash received from customers, which decreases the balance owed.

Accounts receivable processing begins with the balance each customer owed at the start of an accounting period. The amount of each sale on account is added to this balance, and the amount of cash received from each customer is subtracted to arrive at a new balance (Fig. 11-1).

```
      Balance brought forward
   +  Sales on account
   −  Cash receipts
      ─────────────────────
      New balance
```

Figure 11-1.   Calculating balances in accounts receivable.

Accountants use "T" accounts to record business activities and balances. They are called "T" accounts because they resemble the letter T. A "T" account for accounts receivable is illustrated in Fig. 11-2. It shows the original balance brought forward, sales on account, and the new balance on the left (or debit side) of the account. This implies that there was a positive balance in the account at the beginning of the accounting period, that sales on account were added, and that the accounting period concluded with a positive balance in the account.

```
              Accounts Receivable
      ─────────────────────────────────────
      Balance forward at    |
      beginning of period   |
                            |
      Sales on account      | Cash receipts
      for the period        | for the period
      ──────────────────────|
      New balance at end    |
      of period             |
                            |
```

Figure 11-2.   The accounts receivable "T" account.

Cash receipts are shown on the right (or credit side) of the account, indicating that cash received during the accounting period reduced the balance in the account.

In manual accounting, as each transaction occurs, it is recorded in a book of original entry, called a *journal.* Sales on account are recorded in a sales journal and cash receipts in a cash receipts journal. At some point before the accounting period is completed, these transactions are posted in individual accounts. In the accounts receivable process, the individual account for each customer is contained in a book called the *accounts receivable ledger.* The accounts receivable ledger has a T account for each customer. The balance brought forward from the previous period is recorded at the top left side of the account. Sales are recorded on the left side as debits to the account, and cash receipts are recorded on the credit side. The new balance is recorded at the lower left side of the account (Fig. 11-3).

This example considers only the most fundamental transactions. Other possibilities, such as return of merchandise sold, sales discounts, and sales taxes, are disregarded for now. The two fundamental functions in manual accounts receivable are journalizing, which is recording transactions as they occur, and posting, which is recording transactions in the appropriate customer's account. Eventually, the balance in each individual account is determined and listed in a schedule of accounts receivable.

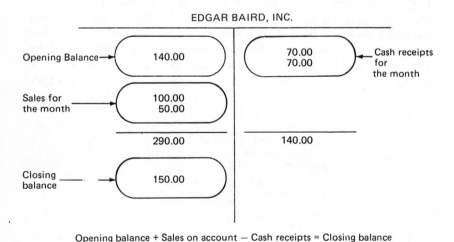

Figure 11-3.   An account in an accounts receivable ledger.

PROCESSING RECEIVABLES BY COMPUTER

When processing receivables by computer, journalizing is accomplished by recording data for each transaction in machine-readable form. In the past, this was done exclusively by keypunching and key verifying, but today any number of input devices, such as optical scanners, key-to-tape, key-to-disk, and terminal input are commonly used. The actual journals are produced by listing the transactions on a printer after they have been proved correct (Fig. 11-4).

Posting, or updating individual accounts, is done by computer. Usually, monthly transactions are sorted by customer number and applied to the existing balance to determine a new balance. Figure 11-5 illustrates the updating of an accounts receivable file, tape master files being used. Output consists of a tape master file containing customer number and balance, and a listing of these balances. The listing of balances is a schedule of accounts receivable (Fig. 11-6).

Recording Sales

Generally, two types of sales transactions exist: cash sales and sales on account. Cash sales are recorded when the cash register tape is balanced with the amount of cash in the register. The company's accounts are updated with a debit, or increase, to the cash account and a credit, also an increase, to the sales account.

Sale of goods on account must be recorded as sales are made. Data concerning a transaction is documented by the salesperson. This document is variously called a sales slip, a sales ticket, or, simply, an order form.

Consider how sales are recorded at the Fenton Mole Sporting Goods Company. At Fenton Mole, a sales slip is completed by the salesperson, itemizing customer name, customer number, item numbers, item descriptions, and quantity sold. The salesperson also assigns an invoice number for the sale. Sales slips are turned in regularly at the sales office or are phoned in when expediting is required.

Fenton Mole has several sales offices throughout the country, each equipped with a terminal connected to the main computer in Dayton, Ohio. Sales of goods on account are recorded at these terminals by a trained clerk who reviews the sales slip, reconciles questionable items, and makes obvious corrections before keying the data. This step is perhaps the most critical in the procedure, since data entered incorrectly at this point will be difficult and expensive to correct later.

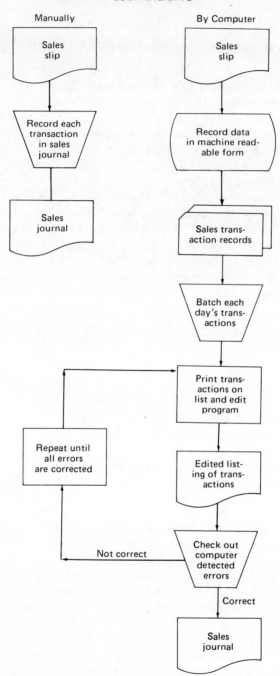

Figure 11-4. Journalizing sales data.

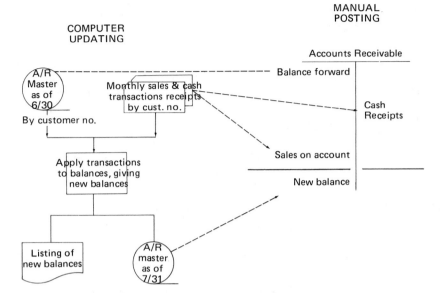

Figure 11-5. Computer updating accounts receivable versus manual posting.

FENTON MOLE CORPORATION
SCHEDULE OF ACCOUNTS RECEIVABLE

AS OF 7/31/79

ACCOUNT NUMBER	ACCOUNT	BALANCE
076	ACE SPORTS	410.50
311	HARTSDALE BLACK SOX	1,418.43
512	DOOLITTLE LEISURE COMPANY	67.00
	TOTAL ACCOUNTS RECEIVABLE	1,895.93

Figure 11-6. A schedule of accounts receivable.

The clerk keys in invoice number, customer number, item number, and quantity of each item sold. The clerk assumes the role of verifier and works with the computer and a visual display unit to insure that the data is recorded correctly.

The computer at Fenton Mole is programmed to receive sales transactions during the hours the sales office is open. The customer master file is on-line with the computer and terminals during these hours. The file contains customer name, street address, city, state, zip code, and the terms of sale normally employed with that customer. It also contains other data, such as credit limits, that may pertain to the sale. The computer system and the clerk interact in this manner:

As the customer number is keyed in, the computer locates the customer's name and address in the customer master file. The computer displays customer name, address, and normal terms used with the customer. This display is checked against the source document, verifying that customer number has been entered correctly into the system. Few things are more disturbing to a customer than to be billed for another customer's purchases. Provision is made for the clerk to override the normal terms of sale when necessary.

The clerk enters item number and quantity sold for each line item contained in the sale. The computer then searches the on-line inventory master file to find the description and unit price for each item. These are displayed along with the extension of price for each item. The clerk compares the descriptions located in the master file with the descriptions on the source document prepared by the salesman. When all are correct, the clerk depresses a key, recording the entire sale onto a disk file located at the main office. Incorrect items are held out until the problems are rectified. (See Fig. 11-7.)

Invoicing

Sales transactions are accumulated each day in a pending invoice file located on disk at the main office in Dayton, Ohio. At the end of each day, and more frequently when required, the file is sorted by invoice number within customer number and is brought on-line with the customer master file and inventory master file for running invoices.

An invoice is notification to a customer of amount owed from a sale. It states the terms of the sale and describes in one line of print the details of each item sold. It also contains the total amount owed as a result of the sale. (See Fig. 11-8.)

An invoice summary record is created on disk as the invoice is printed. It contains invoice number, customer number, and total amount due on the invoice and will be used when the customers'

Courtesy of IBM

Figure 11-7. A station for recording sales on account by typewriter terminal from a sales office.

INVOICE

NUMBER   02735

FENTON MOLE SPORTING GOODS COMPANY
472 APPLE TREE DRIVE
DAYTON, OHIO   45479

SOLD TO

HARVEY'S SPORT SHOP
20 EAST MALL
DAYTON OHIO   45479

DATE: 01/17/79
TERMS: 2/10 NET 30
SHIPPED: EXPRESS

QUANTITY	DESCRIPTION	PRICE	TOTAL
10	MARV THRONEBERRY GLOVES (G1753)	14.95	149.50
12	NATE BOWMAN BASKETBALLS (B0234)	9.95	119.40
100	DICK SHINER FOOTBALLS (F2437)	10.00	1,000.00
	AMOUNT DUE:		1,268.90

Figure 11-8.   An invoice.

account balances are updated. The invoice program also produces an exceptions file, which contains any data that the program is unable to handle. This file is listed and turned over to accounting clerks who reconcile the differences and key in corrections. Invoices affected by these exceptions are run when all required data has been completed.

The result of sales recording and invoicing is that an invoice has been prepared and sent to the customer, the details of that invoice are recorded in the pending invoice file, and a summary of the invoice for use in updating customer balances has been created. (See Fig. 11-9.)

ACCOUNTING FOR CASH RECEIPTS

Cash receipts are a major input into an accounts receivable system. Generally, when cash is received it is deposited in a bank as soon as possible to put the cash to profitable use. The initial steps in handling cash are to verify the amount received, batch the receipts, and deposit.

Cash is normally received in the form of a check accompanied by a document identifying the amount paid. Fenton Mole Sporting Goods Company produces two documents specifying the amount to be paid: an invoice and a monthly statement. The invoice requests payment as the goods are shipped; the statement reminds the customer of all outstanding invoices. Either one may accompany a payment at Fenton Mole.

When payment is received, a clerk compares the amount on the check with the amount on the document and identifies the invoice number paid. Any exception is noted on the document and all unidentified amounts are traced either through looking up company records or calling the customer. Two tasks are then accomplished simultaneously: depositing the checks in the bank and recording the transaction in the company's records. (See Fig. 11-10.)

Bank Deposits

Checks are batched in convenient-sized groups of 50, 100, or a day's transactions. Each batch is totaled on an adding machine for total dollars, and the add tape is retained. Totals of check numbers and customer numbers may be obtained for control purposes. These types of totals are known as *hash totals*. A deposit slip is prepared recording the amount and check number of each item deposited. The bank teller verifies the data in the deposit. The amount deposited becomes a

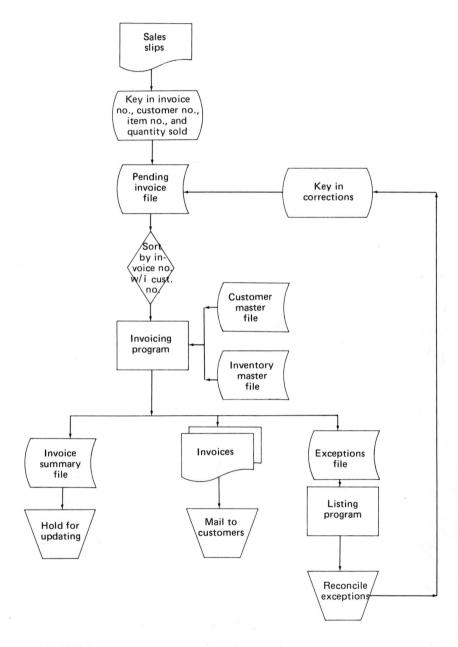

Figure 11-9. Invoicing at Fenton Mole Company.

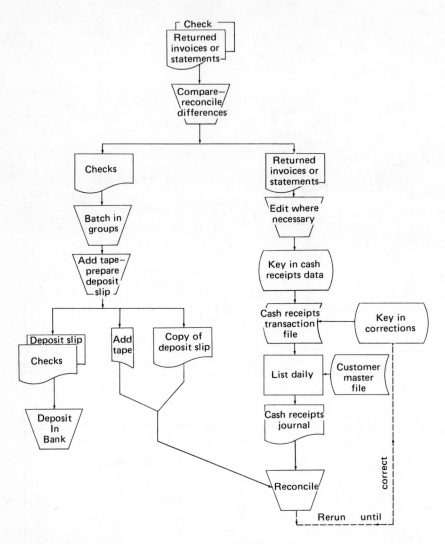

Figure 11-10.   Cash receipts procedure at Fenton Mole Company.

control in the system. The adding machine tape is filed with a copy of the deposit slip for identifying inconsistencies that may arise in the future.

Recording Cash Receipts Transactions

Methods of recording cash receipts vary with the type of input hardware available. If the invoice or monthly statement has been prepared properly, it may be optically scanned. In the past, cash receipt data was keypunched and key verified from source documents. The document describing the amount billed may be on punched cards and, after sight verification, may enter directly into the computer system. Forms that are output from a company's processing system, go to a customer, and return to become input to a system are known as *turn-around documents*.

At Fenton Mole, a clerk enters cash receipt data through a terminal. The clerk records date of transaction, batch number, invoice numbers paid, cash deposited, and customer number. At day's end, cash receipts transactions are listed on the computer and balanced against the adding machine tapes and copies of the deposit slips produced for the deposit. Each batch is balanced and discrepancies are rectified. When required, correcting transactions are keyed into the system; the process is repeated until the totals are correct. The resulting listing is a daily cash receipts journal.

The cash receipts journal is not necessarily correct the first time it is run. Errors are normal at the entry level of a computer system, but they must be detected and corrected as soon as possible. The cash receipts journal is compared with the adding machine tapes of the bank deposits to identify problems. The journal has batch totals for amount deposited, sum of the check numbers, and sum of customer numbers. When inconsistencies appear, a clerk reconciles them and keys in corrections. The journal is rerun until correct.

Updating and Statement Preparation

Preliminary work in the accounts receivable system has produced two transaction files: the summary of current invoices and the cash receipts transaction file. They contain the weekly transactions for the accounts receivable system. Fenton Mole also has a miscellaneous transactions file, which contains all other activities in the accounts receivable system.

All the files are sorted by invoice number within customer number, and put on-line with the customer master file to print a preliminary updating of account balances. The listing is reviewed by clerks who check sample balances against manually established control totals. Errors are corrected by keying in adjusting entries. When the Accounting Department approves a corrected edit listing, the actual file update takes place.

The updating run applies the transactions for the week to the balances contained in the customer master file. The following output is produced:

1. A listing of current balances
2. A disk file containing all overdue accounts
3. A new accounts receivable master file with updated balances

The listing of current balances is distributed to the Accounting and Credit Departments for routine review and action.

The disk file containing a summary of past due accounts is sorted by transaction date within customer number and listed by the schedule of aged accounts receivable program. (See Fig. 11-11.)

Monthly billing statements are run from the updated master file. The billing statement contains a customer's outstanding balance, a listing of each customer's outstanding invoices, their due dates, and the total amount owed.

Other Activities in Accounts Receivable

The summary above is merely a skeleton of the steps taken at the Fenton Mole Company to account for receivables. When the weekly statements have been mailed, each of the files is computer-analyzed and appropriate management reports are produced. Sales data analysis indicates which customers are most profitable, which products are selling, when they are selling, and at what price. Management then can determine what products to maintain in inventory and when and where to anticipate sales.

Other reports point out the comparative effectiveness of salesmen, calculate salesmen's commissions, and indicate for the salesmen which products are the best sellers.

Another series of programs maintains the master files. One program updates price changes in the master inventory file; another makes changes to the customer master file such as adding new customers, changing addresses and terms of sale, and deleting inactive customers.

Many variations exist in the way organizations account for receivables. The system at Fenton Mole using batched input and magnetic disk master files is not particularly sophisticated, but it is typical of many systems employed by small- to medium-sized computer users.

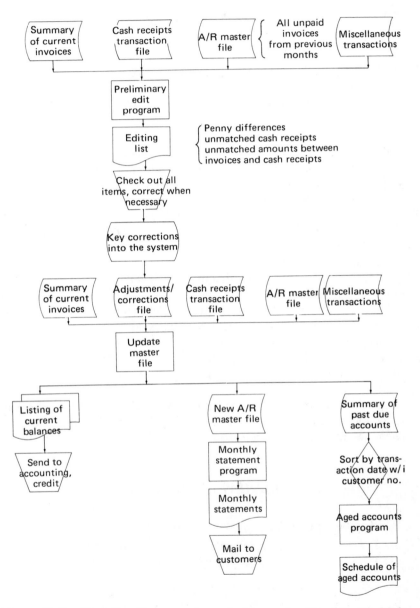

Figure 11-11.   Updating the accounts receivable master file at Fenton Mole Company.

MAKING IT PRACTICAL

Upright Office Furniture Company has had computerized accounts receivable procedures for over 10 years. Its customer master files are on disk packs located at the main office in midtown Manhattan. Upright has five sales and distribution centers, all located within 100 miles of the main office.

Each local office processes over 500 sales per day. Data from these sales is coded, batched, and shipped to the main office weekly along with coding sheets reflecting cash receipts from sales on account. Invoices are prepared manually at the branch offices as each order is shipped.

The status of the customer master file is updated weekly at the main office in New York. Transactions from all the branches are keypunched, key verified, and sorted by customer number to update the account balances. Monthly statements are printed on the computer and sent to each customer with a copy sent to the appropriate branch.

Upright's management feels that the system was adequate when it was installed, but that it has grown obsolete as the company grew and its data processing needs became more complex. Although the entire accounts receivable system is under review, you have been asked to focus your attention on improving the method of preparing data input for sales and cash receipts. "It is time to stop shipping all that paper back and forth," you have been told. "It's time we started using modern methods around here."

Upright is willing to invest whatever is required to install adequate systems for now and well into the foreseeable future. What suggestions do you have for them to improve input preparation?

REVIEW QUESTIONS

1. Briefly explain the process of invoicing.
2. List four ways in which sales on account may be recorded.
3. Explain the function of the T account in accounts receivable.
4. Why is an analysis of aged accounts important to a business?
5. Explain how journalizing is performed by computer.
6. Show the relationship between manual posting and computer updating in accounts receivable.
7. What steps may be taken to improve the accuracy of recording data concerning sales?

8. What does invoicing accomplish? Besides the way it is done at Fenton Mole, describe two other methods of performing invoicing.
9. What function does the billing statement perform? Where does it differ from the invoice?
10. Explain the controls used by Fenton Mole in verifying its cash receipts.

GLOSSARY

Aged Accounts—past due receivable accounts

Accounts Receivable—the process of recording the amount due a company from sales on account

Accounts Receivable Ledger—a book that contains the balances and activities of a company's sales on account

Cash Receipts Journal—a listing of an organization's cash receipts as they occur

Credit—an entry on the right side of an account

Debit—an entry on the left side of an account

Hash Totals—totals of any number in a record for control purposes

Journal—a chronological listing of transactions; an accounting book for the original recording of transactions

Journalizing—entering transactions in a journal

Posting—recording transactions in a ledger

Sales Slip—a document for recording the details of a sale

Sale on Account—a sale in which the buyer has a period of time to pay for the merchandise

Schedule of Accounts Receivable—a listing of customer balances

T Account—a device for recording the activity and balance of an account

Transaction—a business event that requires recording

Turn-around Document—a document that originates in an organization, leaves it, and eventually reenters it as input into a system

12

Computerized Inventory

Objectives

This chapter explains how another of the basic accounting processes is performed with computers. Various types of inventory maintenance are examined, and sample computerized inventory systems, common to many types of business, are presented. The student should gain a general idea of the importance of computerized inventory maintenance and grasp how it is done in many businesses.

INVENTORY SYSTEMS

Types of Inventory

The process of determining the number and cost of the items that an organization has in stock is called inventory. Two methods for determining inventory are *periodic,* in which at some point in time each item is physically counted, and *perpetual,* in which the amount of each transaction is added to or subtracted from the item count as it occurs. Periodic inventories have always been commonplace. A business takes stock of merchandise at the end of a fiscal year to determine its cost and eventually its affect upon the organization's net income. Before computers were used, perpetual inventory was cumbersome and usually impractical. Today, many organizations who have successfully installed a computer maintain perpetual inventory of their stock and verify the accuracy of this data with periodic physical inventories.

Inventory is a broad term that includes a variety of applications. Retail stores and wholesale distributors must keep track of merchandise available for their customers. A bank maintains an inventory of account balances; an airline, reservations; an insurance company, policy status. All follow the same general principles of inventory maintenance.

The Importance of Inventory

Controlling inventory is vital to most organizations. Maintaining inventory is an expense which of itself earns nothing. Storing and insuring goods is expensive, as is discarding them when they have spoiled or become obsolete. Moreover, capital tied up in excessive inventory can be used for more profitable investment. But it is expensive also to lose a customer because an item is not in stock. This cost becomes more severe when that customer takes his future business to a competitor. Ideally, a company should have on hand exactly enough inventory to satisfy its customers' needs. Determining the customers' needs precisely is one area in which computer systems assist corporate decision making.

A Simplified Inventory System

Maintaining a perpetual inventory entails keeping track of the quantity of all items in stock. Essentially, inventory balances increase when items are purchased, and they are decreased by sales. Other events affecting inventory balances—sales and purchases returns, spoilage, pilferage, and discarding obsolete items—are handled as adjustments to inventory.

A physical inventory of item number and amount on hand is taken to establish a perpetual inventory. This data is recorded in machine-readable form and listed for verification. When the file is affirmed as being accurate and up-to-date, perpetual inventory maintenance may begin.

Sales and adjustments regularly deplete inventory balances for each item to the point where each item must be reordered before the supply of the item is exhausted. Sufficient lead time is provided to allow the quantity ordered to arrive before the item is out of stock. Terms commonly used in inventory processing include:

reorder point   the level for each item at which the stock must be replenished

reorder amount   the quantity of each item which must be ordered to satisfy demand

capacity   the maximum quantity of an item that can be stored economically

Figure 12-1 shows the elementary functions of stock maintenance. Beginning inventory for an accounting period is established with a physical inventory. The item is reordered when stock is depleted below the established reorder point. Quantity reordered depends upon several factors: continued demand for the product, price, and storage capacity available. The illustration indicates that reorders are for the full amount that can be stored. When the accounting cycle is completed, normally at the close of a fiscal year, a physical inventory verifies quantity on hand.

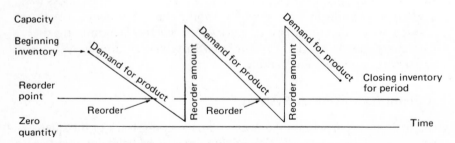

Figure 12-1. Elementary functions of inventory.

Computerized Inventory

Computerized inventories are perpetual; every addition to and deletion from stock is recorded in machine-readable form, and the quantity on hand for each item is updated regularly. Some organizations require only weekly or monthly status updating, but daily or more frequent updating is common. When an organization requires exact information on stock status, inventory is updated in a real-time environment.

Computer-based inventory systems still require physical inventories. However, in a perpetual system, the physical inventory can be taken when convenient; perhaps one-twelfth of it can be done each month, or it may be scheduled when slack time exists.

Input to computerized inventory systems is normally a by-product from another system. Sales invoices that are input to accounts receivable are also used to delete items from stock. Accounts payable invoices are the primary source for adding quantities to stock.

Figure 12-2 shows a very fundamental inventory system using a magnetic tape master file and punched card transactions. This primitive system is designed to keep track of the quantity on hand for each item and provide some statistical data.

Input comes from three general sources: accounts receivable invoices for stock deletions, accounts payable invoices for additions to stock, and adjustment coding sheets. Adjustments include cash sales, cash purchases, and adjustments resulting from physical inventories. The source documents are keypunched, key verified, and sorted by item number, the sequence of the magnetic tape master file. Before updating, the transactions are listed with an editing program and all questionable transactions are checked out and corrected. Updating is accomplished when both files, the punched card transactions and the magnetic tape masters, are processed in item number order. Transactions are applied to the corresponding master records, resulting in an updated master record for each item. The output master file is simultaneously listed, producing the current file status for reference.

Most organizations require far more from an inventory system than the one above provides. For instance:

1. Amount on order must be added to amount on hand to determine whether there is sufficient supply of the product to satisfy demand.
2. The computer system should notify the user when to reorder each item and, in a sophisticated system, print the purchase order.

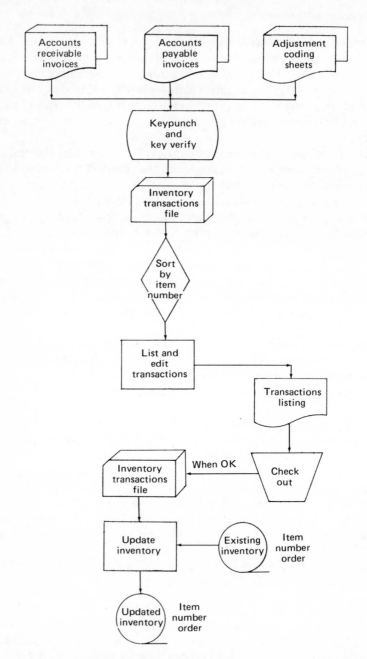

Figure 12-2. An inventory system using a magnetic tape master file.

3. The reordering run may also calculate the most economical lot to order, provided that the complexities required for that decision have been programmed.
4. Ultimately, the system should provide an analysis of the demand for each product so that future stock needs may be forecast.
5. The system should provide follow-up on items that have been ordered but shipment has not been received within a reasonable period of time and on those for which the quantity on hand has fallen below a safe level.

Figures 12-3 and 12-4 illustrate a disk-oriented inventory system that incorporates these features.

Fawcett and Leake Corporation, wholesalers in plumbing and heating equipment, installed the system illustrated in Fig. 12-3 and 12-4 over three years ago. Fawcett and Leake has its main office in Quincy, Massachusetts and has warehouses and distribution facilities in Brockton, Marlboro, Salem, East Boston, Concord, and Quincy, Massachusetts. Each of the branches has teleprocessing facilities for keying in transactions and inquiries, and each uses CRT displays for verifying input and receiving answers to inquiries.

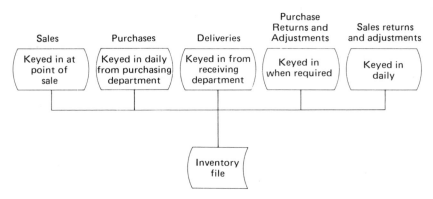

Figure 12-3. An inventory system with the master file on-line for updating.

Five types of input transactions affecting inventory are used:

1. *Sales*
   Both sales on account and cash sales are keyed in from the branch making the sale. The transmission sets up a record for printing invoices as it deletes the items sold from stock when the goods are shipped.

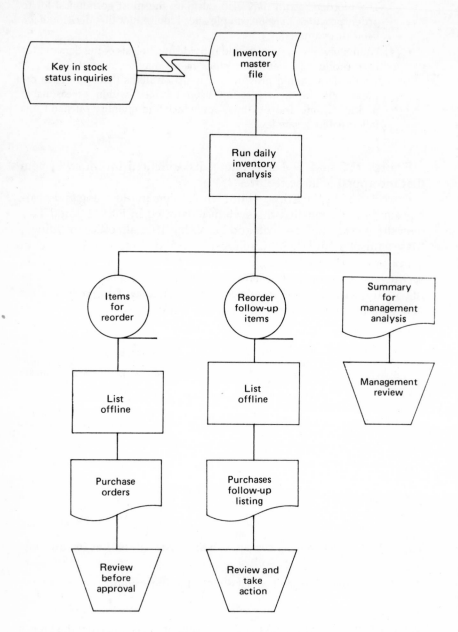

Figure 12-4.   Daily activity of disk-oriented real-time inventory master file.

2. *Purchases*

   All purchases are channeled through the Purchasing Department located at the main office in Quincy. As items are approved for purchase, the quanity ordered and the item number are recorded as on order in the master inventory file.

3. *Deliveries*

   The Receiving Department of each branch completes an item receipt ticket for each item received. These tickets are picked up twice a day at each branch and delivery data keyed into the inventory file, changing the status of items from on order to on hand.

4. *Purchases Returns*

   Returns of purchases and deletions from stock discovered during physical inventories are keyed in from each branch when required.

5. *Sales Returns*

   Sales returns and additions to stock resulting from physical inventories are keyed in from each branch when required.

The inventory master file is on-line for receiving input from all branches throughout the working day. The organization records all transactions within eight hours after they occur, but does not attempt to maintain a real-time file.

Figure 12-4 shows the output that the inventory master file provides daily. First, the file is on-line during the working day for stock inventory status on all items carried. This is particularly important when one branch is out of an item but can locate it at another branch and complete the sale.

At the end of each day, the inventory master file is processed with a daily inventory analysis program that produces this output:

1. A magnetic tape file is written that contains items for reorder. Reorder points and economic ordering lots have been determined for each product monthly. The tape file for items to reorder is used to print purchase orders off-line on a small computer each day. The purchase orders are reviewed by the Purchasing Department and approved when a purchase should be made.

2. Items that fall below a critical level or are on order for more than four weeks are written on magnetic tape. The tape is listed off-line daily and required follow-up action is taken.

3. The daily program also provides management with a summary of stock status, listing information that management has previously defined as important to stock management.

MAKING IT PRACTICAL

You are the executive vice-president of Tubbs and Faucett, a distributor of plumbing parts in the greater Philadelphia area. Tubbs and Faucett purchases plumbing parts from manufacturers and sells them to building contractors and plumbers. It stocks over 10,000 parts and has considerable stock duplication among its four branches located within 30 miles of the main office. The organization has decided to install a computer to coordinate inventory management.

You have specified that an up-to-date, meaningful inventory system would be the most critical part of the proposed computer installation. In a recent memo, you stated, "We must know what we have in stock and what we are doing with that stock so that we can reduce inventory and satisfy our customers better."

The data processing department has asked you to make a list of five reports that you will require from the new system. Specify the name of the report, its frequency, give a brief explanation of its contents, and state how it will be used to benefit the company.

REVIEW QUESTIONS

1. Distinguish between perpetual and periodic inventories.
2. Why is it feasible to do perpetual inventory by computer but normally impractical to do it manually?
3. Comment on this statement: Maintaining excessive inventory wastes an organization's capital.
4. Why do computer-based inventory systems still require physical inventories?
5. Why types of transactions create input to an inventory system?
6. List four goals that an organization usually expects its computerized inventory system to accomplish.
7. What advantages do disk inventory systems have over those that use magnetic tape as the basic storage medium?
8. How is a computerized perpetual inventory system started?

GLOSSARY

Inventory—the process of determining the number and cost of items that an organization has in stock

Periodic Inventory—physically counting items in stock at some point in time

Perpetual Inventory—adding or subtracting the amount of each transaction as it occurs

Physical Inventory—manually counting stock items

Reorder Amount—the quantity of each item that must be ordered to satisfy demand

Reorder Point—the level for each item at which the stock must be replenished

13

Payroll and Payable Systems

Objectives

This chapter presents two more elementary computer applications. The systems presented are generalized, and are not designed for any particular organization. The student is expected to gain a deeper realization of how the computer is used at a fundamental level in business.

COMPONENTS OF A PAYROLL SYSTEM

Payroll is the most universal data processing application; it is a function performed with the same basic steps in most organizations. An automated payroll is usually justified when a company's staff exceeds 100 employees.

Primary output from a payroll system includes payroll checks, government reports—especially the annual W-2 report on wages paid and withheld, and the quarterly 941-A withholding report—and statistical reports of labor distribution, financial planning, and job costing.

A payroll master file contains permanent information about each employee. The file must be updated each pay period for status changes, new employees, and for employees leaving the company. Figure 13-1 illustrates a typical payroll master record. This record is comparatively simple, designed to produce only essential payroll output. If more complex reports were required, the record layout would be more extensive.

Changes to payroll systems include status changes in the master file, such as changes in number of dependents, name changes, pay increases, additions to and deletions from file, and changes in deduction amounts. The basic transaction in a payroll system is the recording of hours worked during the current pay period for hourly personnel. Salaried employees require no input transaction during a normal pay period.

MAINTAINING THE MASTER FILE

The payroll master file consists of one record for each active employee in an organization. In a company that pays weekly, this file is updated each week for additions, deletions, and changes. A new master record is created for each employee who enters the payroll system and a transaction is entered to delete employees who are leaving. Every change in status requires a transaction. A week's transactions are batched, and controls are established for such items as number of employees, total salary, total wages for hourly personnel, total number of dependents, and whatever else is required to insure accuracy. The changes are computer-edited, and the file with the changes included is listed and its updated status compared with the established controls. Inconsistencies are reconciled. When the file is correct, it is held for the weekly paying procedure (Fig. 13-2).

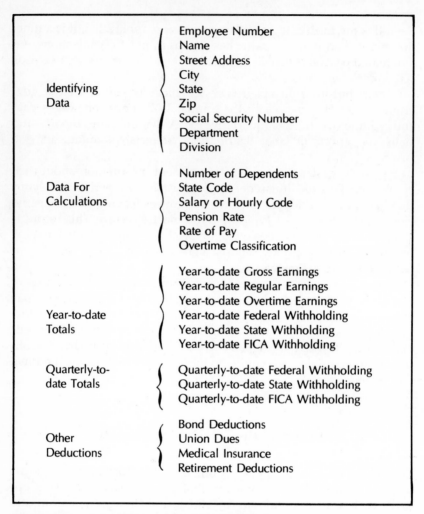

Figure 13-1.   A typical payroll master record.

PAYING THE STAFF

Business organizations pay employees weekly, semi-monthly, bi-weekly, and occasionally monthly. The examples in this chapter use a weekly payroll. Figure 13-3 illustrates a typical system for weekly payroll.

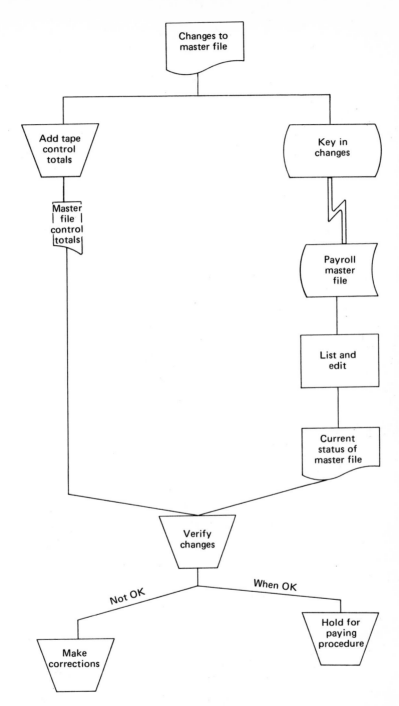

Figure 13-2. Updating the payroll file.

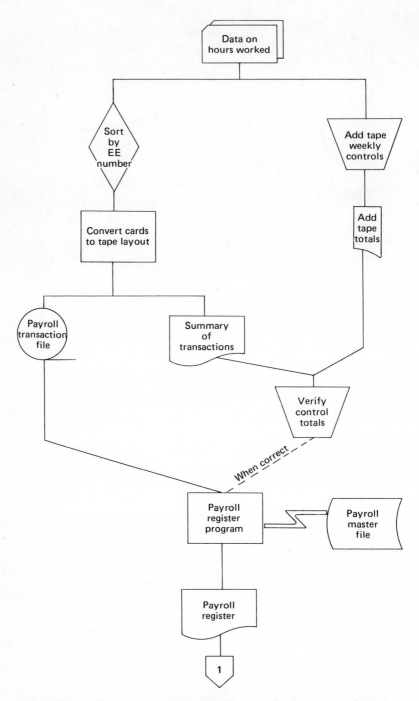

Figure 13-3.   Weekly payroll procedure.

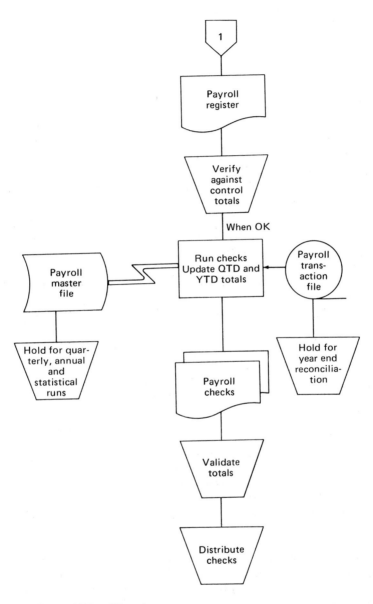

Figure 13-3. *(Cont.)*

For payroll purposes, an organization's staff is divided into two categories: hourly personnel, who receive a fixed rate per hour and an additional rate after a certain number of hours (usually time and a half after 35 or 40 hours), and salaried employees, who receive $\frac{1}{52}$ of an annual salary each week. No input data is required for salaried employees, unless a status change has occurred during the week. The hours worked for hourly personnel are recorded each week on a time clock or clerically, and converted to machine-readable form. The transactions in Fig. 13-3 are shown as punched card records. Control totals are established for the transactions, which are then sorted by employee number. (Many organizations use the social security number as the employee number.) The transactions are processed with a program that converts the cards to magnetic tape format for quicker handling later. The program also summarizes control totals for the transactions. The totals are compared with the adding machine tape control totals previously established to verify that the tape records represent the actual hours worked by the employees. When the transactions are correct, a payroll register is run.

A payroll register is a preliminary run of the actual payroll checks. It calculates net pay for each staff member with this formula:

$$\text{Gross pay} - \text{Deductions} = \text{Net pay}$$

For salaried employees in a weekly payroll, gross pay is $\frac{1}{52}$ of gross annual salary. Hourly gross pay for employees who earn time and a half after 40 hours is calculated:

IF HOURS WORKED LESS THAN OR EQUAL TO 40:
      Gross salary = hourly rate × hours worked

IF HOURS WORKED GREATER THAN 40:
Subtract 40 from hours worked, obtaining overtime hours
Multiply hourly rate by 40
Multiply overtime hours by (hourly rate × 1.5)

Deductions are subtracted from weekly gross pay. Deductions include federal, state, and city withholding tax, FICA withholding, Blue Cross-Blue Shield payments, major medical payments, union dues, retirement pension payments, bonds, voluntary charitable contributions, disability insurance payments, loan repayments, and garnishees.

The primary output from this run is the payroll register. The register is actually a listing of the checks and employees' payroll statements on standard printer paper. The run also contains control totals to be verified by the clerical staff to insure the accuracy of all items in the payroll. When the register is verified and approved, the computer operations department is authorized to run weekly payroll checks. (See Fig. 13-4.)

		EARNINGS						
NAME	TOTAL HOURS	REG	OT	TOTAL	YTD EARNINGS	FICA DED	FED WITH	NET PAY
CHAPMAN	42	200.00	15.00	215.00	4,025.16	12.58	36.00	166.50
DANIELS	35	175.00	.00	175.00	2,075.00	10.24	17.50	147.26
SCANLON	50	200.00	75.00	275.00	3,085.00	15.99	41.75	217.26
MCCABE	42	160.00	12.00	172.00	1,976.43	9.05	16.24	146.71

DIPACE ENTERPRISES
PAYROLL REGISTER

Figure 13-4.   A payroll register.

The check-writing run also produces control totals to verify that nothing has changed since the payroll register has been run. As a by-product of this run, quarterly-to-date and year-to-date totals are updated in the master file. The payroll transaction tape is held for any statistical and balancing runs that may be required in the future.

REQUIRED GOVERNMENT REPORTS

The system outlined in this chapter maintains quarterly-to-date and year-to-date accumulations in the master file. Many companies maintain this data in separate summary files. Each quarter, companies are required to report on wages paid and amount withheld for that quarter to the federal government. A quarterly program will produce this report, 941-A from the master file. The program also resets all quarterly-to-date totals to zero. The annual W-2 report of wages paid and withheld is similarly run from the master file with all year-to-date totals being reset to zero.

Payroll files usually contain more data than is indicated in this chapter. Payroll files are often combined with personnel information to provide data for various statistical and budgetary reports helpful to management. It is in the area of statistical reports that payroll systems differ from one organization to another.

ACCOUNTS PAYABLE PROCESSING

Accounts payable is the process of recording and paying for purchases on account. The sample computerized accounts payable system outlined below is frequently used in retail and wholesale operations where merchandise for resale is purchased on account. When one company has an account with another, they agree upon credit terms for each sale. Typical credit terms are 2/10 net 30, meaning that if the purchaser pays within 10 days he may take a 2 percent discount, but he must pay the balance within 30 days. Under these terms, any invoice not paid within 30 days is past due.

In accounts payable, an organization must know the amount to pay, the invoice's due date, and the final date in which a discount can be claimed. Figure 13-5 illustrates a computerized system that provides this basic information.

In the flowchart, two different documents are the sources for transactions in the system. Data from purchase orders, the forms used by the purchaser to initiate and obtain approval for a purchase, is keyed into a disk file to create a pending order file. This data includes purchase order number, vendor number, items purchased and their quantities, and the date of the transaction. The sales invoice received from the seller notifying the purchaser of the items bought and amount owed also provides input data. Invoice date, terms of sale, vendor number, purchase order number, if available, and invoice number are recorded in an accounts payable pending invoice file. Both purchase order and invoice data are keyed in daily. Each day both files are sorted by vendor number and processed with a program which compares the transactions in the pending order file with those in the accounts payable pending invoice file. The program does the following:

1. Deletes from the pending order file all purchase orders for which invoices have been received.
2. Lists for review all transactions that have been in the pending order file for an unusual period, perhaps 15 days.
3. Lists all invoices received for which no purchase order exists.
4. Creates a file of accounts payable pending invoices.

Accounts payable pending invoices to be paid become input to another system, which verifies that the items have been received before authorizing payment.

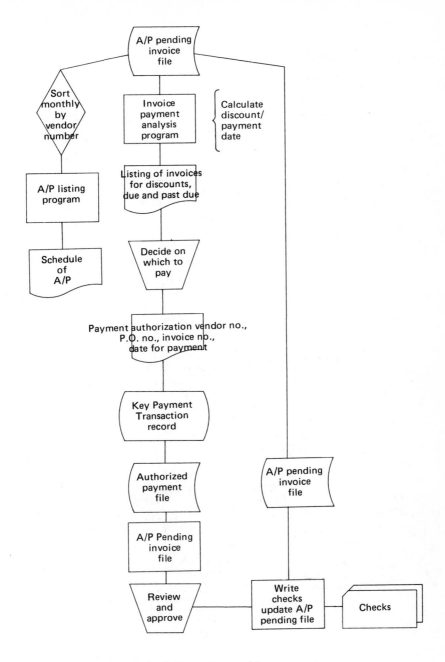

Figure 13-5.   Computerized accounts payable.

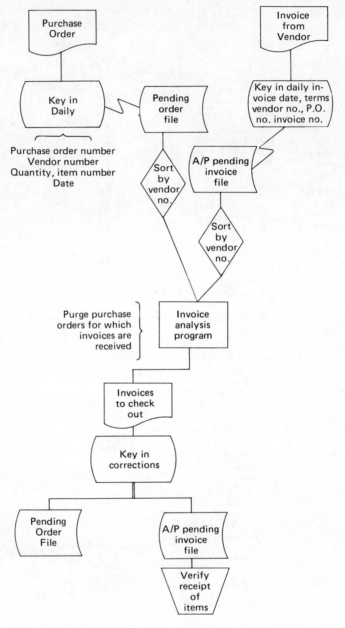

Figure 13-5. *(Cont.)*

260

The accounts payable pending invoice file contains one record for each invoice a company owes. The company must decide whether to pay each invoice within the discount period, before the due date, or at some other time. These decisions depend on such factors as the organization's available cash, the terms of the purchase, and corporate policy on cash discounts. When these factors are relatively stable, they are programmed, and the computer makes these routine decisions.

The accounts payable pending invoice file is processed by a payments analysis program, which calculates the last day for paying within the discount period, the discount, the net amount due, and when to pay the invoice. This data is listed by invoice number and presented for authorization to the person responsible (Fig. 13-6).

ANALYSIS OF ACCOUNTS PAYABLE

ACCOUNT	AMOUNT PAYABLE	DISCOUNT DATE	DISCOUNT RATE	DISCOUNTED AMOUNT TO PAY	NORMAL DUE DATE
BYRNE BROTHERS	250.00	3/07	2%	245.00	3/27
NELSON INC	400.00	3/09	2%	392.00	3/29
BALLOU ASSOC	300.00	3/10	1%	297.00	3/25

Figure 13-6. An analysis of accounts payable.

Ultimately, no matter how thoroughly the computer has been programmed, a person decides which invoices to pay and which to delay. Approval for payment of an invoice is recorded by keying in invoice numbers of invoices to be paid. The resulting authorized payment file is processed with the accounts payable pending invoice file to produce a check register for invoice payment. The check register is reviewed, and, if correct, approved by the person responsible before checks are run. The check-writing program updates the accounts payable pending invoice file, leaving in it invoices which have not been approved for payment.

MAKING IT PRACTICAL

A business enterprise is often considered as one integrated system rather than as a series of unrelated systems. In a wholesale distributor, for instance, a purchase not only establishes an account payable for a company, but also increases inventory balances. A sale on account establishes an account receivable, while it decreases inventory status.

Bob Sawyer, the general manager of Chatham Electronics, has been giving some thought as to how his business systems are organized. Chatham purchases electrical equipment from over 200 manufacturers and stores it in its one warehouse location. It distributes this equipment to retail outlets, electricians, and construction contractors. Chatham currently has over 8000 different items in stock.

Mr. Sawyer has asked you to draw a chart for him showing how accounts payable, accounts receivable, inventory, and cash receipts and payments systems are related in his business. Draw this chart for him.

REVIEW QUESTIONS

1. Give three examples of output from a payroll system.
2. Give some examples of status changes to a payroll master file.
3. What two basic reports are required by the United States federal government from a payroll system?
4. How is salary for hourly personnel calculated?
5. What is meant by the term 1/10 net 60?
6. What information must an accounts payable system provide?
7. Upon what criteria does a company base its decision on whether to pay an invoice within the discount period?
8. Why are quarterly-to-date and year-to-date totals accumulated in a payroll master file?
9. What processing differences exist between hourly and salaried employees?
10. Besides the items listed in Fig. 13-1, what other fields would you include in a payroll master file?

GLOSSARY

Accounts Payable—the process of recording and paying for purchases on account

Cash Discount—a discount allowed for early payment of an invoice

Due Date—the last day a payable may be paid on time

Payroll Register—a preliminary listing of the checks that will be paid in a payroll system

Purchase Order—a source document for initiating and obtaining approval for a purchase

14

The Computer and the Marketing Function

Objectives

When basic accounting systems are installed and operating satisfactorily, an organization uses the data these systems provide to improve its marketing activities. This chapter explains how three marketing functions—sales forecasting, distribution, and new product development—are supported by the computer.

THE COMPUTER AND MARKETING

Marketing includes development, pricing, promotion, and distribution of products. Data processing systems in today's business organizations provide much of the information required to perform each of these functions effectively. Moreover, the computer provides the potential for analyzing marketing information so that marketing management can consistently make profitable decisions concerning product line.

The decision maker in today's marketing environment not only has the computing ability of data processing equipment available, but with direct access and teleprocessing terminals, he can locate pertinent data immediately, analyze it, and make a quick, intelligent decision. The computer is no longer a remote device to be entrusted solely to data processing professionals; today's computer is readily available to the non-EDP manager.

Although the computer is important to many aspects of marketing, this chapter will deal with only a few of them: sales forecasting, product distribution, and controlling new product development.

SALES FORECASTING FOR EXISTING PRODUCTS

Perhaps the most critical item for a company to know is its volume of future sales. When future sales are known with reasonable accuracy, a company can plan personnel and training requirements, capital outlay, and purchasing, production, and distribution needs. Future sales can only be estimated; they can never actually be known. Planning is based upon well-defined goals; the more accurately the goals are defined, the better the possibility for developing sound plans.

Fundamental accounting systems in any organization—accounts receivable, accounts payable, inventory, and payroll—provide marketing data as a natural by-product. Accounts receivable systems contain data on past sales, the starting point for projecting future sales.

Since a normal accounting cycle is one month, a month's sales usually are used for developing sales statistics. A relationship exists between June sales and anticipated sales for July, but this is certainly not a one-for-one relationship. June may be a peak sales month for a product; July a slump month. Sales for a particular product may be declining steadily, and June sales may merely indicate that July sales will be even worse. June may have 22 business days in it; July only 21.

Sales for one month must be adjusted before they can be used as a guide for projecting next month's sales.

Marketing managers use statistical models for evaluating the effect of past sales on future performance of a product. A model uses mathematical values to represent real business situations. It is a business problem expressed in equation form. The advantage of a mathematical model is that each of the components in the model can be easily changed and new values tested. Moreover, the model can be computer-programmed so that thousands of possibilities can be tested in a relatively brief period of time.

A simple mathematical model permits past sales to be adjusted for various factors to predict future sales. The equation below serves as the starting point for a model.

$$\text{June sales (adjusted)} = \text{July sales}$$

Marketing management must establish the amount of the adjustment. If the only factor differentiating June sales from July sales were that there are 21 business days in July and 22 in June, and all other factors were equal, the equation would read:

$$\text{June sales} \times 0.95454 = \text{July sales}$$

Realistically, the relationship between one month's sales of a product and another's is never so simple. Instead of merely taking one month's sales data, it would be more meaningful to take the most recent three or four month's sales and modify them by the number of business days in each month. If the norm were 21 days per month, and April had 21, May, 20, and June, 22 days, the equation would read:

$$\frac{\text{Apr. sales } (1.00000) + \text{May sales } (1.05000) + \text{June sales } (0.95454) = \text{July sales}}{3}$$

Products that have been on the market for some time have accumulated sales data for several years. It is possible to develop average monthly sales for that product for a two-year period, but even that average is deceiving. Sales in more recent months are more significant than sales a year and a half ago. Sales on many items are seasonal. Sales for last August are probably more meaningful in determining this August's sales than this year's April sales. Each month's sales must be given a weight in proportion with its importance in the equation. A more realistic equation is:

$$\frac{\text{Month 1 sales}^* + \text{Month 2 sales}^* \ldots + \ldots \text{Month 24 sales}^*}{24} = \begin{array}{c}\text{forecasted} \\ \text{monthly} \\ \text{sales}\end{array}$$

This equation includes only the most fundamental adjusting factors. A realistic sales forecast is much more complex.

This equation could possibly be solved manually, even if several more factors were applied to each month's sales. However, in practice, a computer is needed because:

1. The calculations above are performed for one product; most companies have hundreds of products for which sales must be forecast.
2. In realistic situations, the factors affecting sales projections are more complex than indicated here.
3. Sales forecasting is an ongoing process. Static averages used here must give way to moving averages in which the months included in the equation constantly change, a process too cumbersome for manual calculations.
4. Computer systems provide continual feedback on how forecasted sales compare with actual sales. The marketing manager receives data regularly to evaluate the effect of each of the factors in the forecast. Factors are constantly revised until the forecasts are consistently accurate. Even then, results must still be monitored and factors reevaluated to keep pace with the effects changing business conditions have on products.

FORECASTING SALES FOR NEW PRODUCTS

If the basic factor in forecasting sales for an existing product is past sales, what data can be used for predicting sales on a new product for which no prior sales data exists? Factors are available from which an

---

*Adjusted for number of business days, season, and timeliness. '

initial model may be formed. For example, figures on the gross national product (GNP), unemployment, discretionary income, housing starts, and rate of inflation are available and are important components in determining potential demand for a new product. Each can be quantified, and, in light of past experience, their effect on the future sales of the new product can be estimated. Although they are only estimates, estimates are far better than no data for a starting point, and eventually these estimates can be refined into a smooth-working model. Companies forecast sales for a new product by first developing a model for all new products and improving this model as each new product is developed, until the model produces satisfactory results.

The initial step in forecasting sales on a new product is to formulate a list of all known factors affecting the sale of that product. In addition to those mentioned above, a company normally would have information on:

1. The effects of past advertising campaigns on sales
2. Market share of existing company products
3. Sales tax rates in specific locales and their effects on the sale of specific products
4. First year's versus subsequent years' performance of products
5. Competitors' reactions to new product introduction

The impact of these factors and many more are estimated and expressed in a mathematical equation. The equation is at best crude, but it serves as a starting point for developing a working model. The objective of building this preliminary model is to predict a rough estimate of the demand for the developing product.

Simultaneously with construction of the model, the new product is market-tested under controlled conditions in several geographic areas. When the model has been constructed, it is tested with a series of prepared cases, and the results of the test are compared with the results of the market tests. Obvious flaws in the equation are corrected, and new and better estimates are derived. Factors with a high degree of predictability are even more precisely defined. The model is retested against the pretested data until the results are reasonable. Ultimately, the model will produce estimated annual and monthly sales.

Budget, personnel, production, training, distribution, and purchasing plans are formulated on the basis of these projections. When the product is finally on the market, its monthly sales are compared with each month's forecasted sales and annual sales are compared with forecasted annual sales. The model is further refined, and each input factor is evaluated as to its effectiveness in predicting sales. The model serves a dual function at this point; it is used for predicting future sales of the new product, and it is being honed for use for forecasting sales on all future new products.

The primary benefit of developing a model for evaluating potential sales for a new product is that a model is created that can be used in appraising the potential of future new products. The model must be refined as new circumstances arise, but its existence is significant, and it will continue to provide meaningful information on future new products.

THE MARKETING MANAGER
AND THE
MARKETING MODEL

A key task of the marketing manager is to determine emerging trends in the sales of existing products and make correct decisions based upon these trends. Sales data, properly processed, will show the products whose sales are starting to falter. One option of the marketing manager is to decide whether the product should be dropped or supported with a stepped-up promotional campaign. To do this, the decision maker must understand what trends the data is indicating. For example, climate influences long-term sales on snow tires; a week of snowy weather will influence the short-term trend. Although a computer can access an incredible amount of data and process it at unimaginable speeds, some data cannot be quantified and thus cannot be handled by the computer. This qualitative information is available to the decision maker, and he must apply this knowledge to the computer output to make profitable decisions. What the computer can do, however, is, over a period of time, measure the effects that these human decisions have upon future sales of the product. Human judgment, however, will always take precedence over the computer's output.

THE COMPUTER AND PRODUCT DISTRIBUTION

One marketing application in which the power of the computer has been successfully used is the distribution of products to retail outlets and warehouse storage. A statistical model, generally known as the Transportation Problem, illustrates the basic principles used in computerized distribution. Consider this simplification of the problem and the techniques used:

The Fenton Mole Sporting Goods Company manufactures baseball bats at two factories. The bats are transported to each of two warehouses, where they are distributed to retailers.

The plant in Doubleday produces 7000 bats per day; the plant in Cobbsville manufactures 3000. Demand for bats at the Eastern and Western warehouses is 5000 each per day. It costs $100 to ship 1000 bats from Doubleday to the Eastern warehouse, and $90 to the Western warehouse. To ship 1000 bats from Cobbsville to Eastern costs $80, and from Cobbsville to Western costs $95. Graphically, the problem looks as shown in Fig. 14-1.

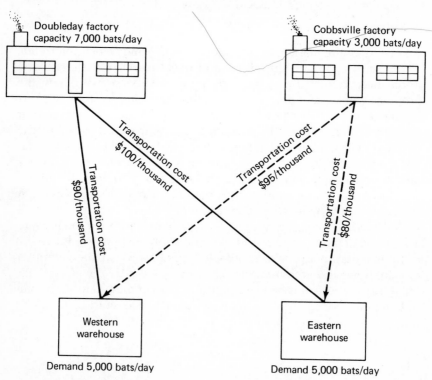

Figure 14-1.

With a little thought, the solution to the problem is obvious. Doubleday has the greater capacity of the two plants and it ships bats $10 cheaper per thousand to Western than to Eastern. Thus, if it sent Western its full capacity of bats, 5000, Western would require no shipment from Cobbsville. Cobbsville's full capacity of 3000 bats would go to Eastern, which would receive the remaining 2000 bats from Doubleday.

In practice, more variables usually exist. There may be 12 factories and 30 warehouses, and the transportation cost among the various combinations may vary widely. The transportation problem must then be solved by computer program using the same logic that we used to solve the simple problem illustrated above.

To organize a solution to this problem, establish a matrix with the points of origin listed down the left side and the destinations across the top. The cost for each combination is written in a square in the upper left-hand corner of each box in the matrix in Fig. 14-2.

		Destinations	
		Western	Eastern
Points of origin	Doubleday	90 A	100 B
	Cobbsville	95 C	80 D

Figure 14-2.

In this problem there are only four possible combinations for shipment between point of origin and destination, which we will call A, B, C, and D. The matrix is completed by putting in the column totals (demand) for each destination and the row totals for the capacity of each point of origin (Fig. 14-3). Examine the illustration until you are convinced that these equations are correct:

$$A + B = 7000$$
$$C + D = 3000$$
$$A + C = 5000$$
$$B + D = 5000$$

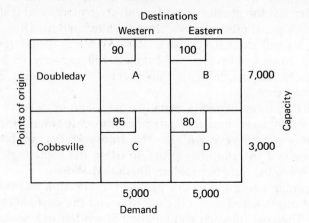

Figure 14-3.

An initial solution for the problem is formulated and tested for cost. The standard method for determining an initial solution is to ship as much as possible from the first point of origin to the first destination. In the problem, Western can handle a maximum of 5000 bats per day, so that is the quantity shipped from Doubleday. The remaining production of the Doubleday plant, 2000 bats, must go to Eastern (Fig. 14-4). The entire shipment from Cobbsville must then go to Eastern. This combination would cost:

Doubleday to Western: 5000 bats × $90 per thousand = $4500
Doubleday to Eastern: 2000 bats × $100 per thousand = $2000
Cobbsville to Western: 0 bats × $95 per thousand = $ 0
Cobbsville to Eastern: 3000 bats × $80 per thousand = $2400

We know that one possible solution to the problem would cost $8900, but the best solution is desired. To find it, each possible solution is tested. Assuming that the bats are shipped in cartons of 1000, we then change the quantity in the upper left sector of the matrix. The solution (Fig. 14-5) would be

4000 bats × $90 per thousand = $3600
3000 bats × $100 per thousand = $3000
1000 bats × $95 per thousand = $ 950
2000 bats × $80 per thousand = $1600
                                ――――――
                                 $9150

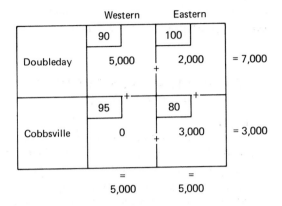

Figure 14-4. Initial solution.

All possible solutions to the matrix must be tested similarly. It happens that in this problem the initial solution is the optimum one.

The value of this tool to the marketing manager is that the logic of the matrix and its arithmetic functions can be programmed so that far more involved matrices can be quickly solved. The marketing manager must define the origins, destinations, production capacities, demands, and transportation cost figures. He must understand the functions of the program and provide the program with the most accurate data available.

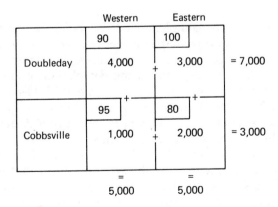

Figure 14-5. Second feasible solution.

The transportation problem illustrated is so simple that it can be solved manually. But when there are 20 manufacturing sites and 10 warehouses, computer programs must be used.

CONTROLLING NEW PRODUCT DEVELOPMENT

Bringing a new product to the consumer requires management coordination throughout the entire organization. PERT (Project Evaluation and Review Technique) is a management tool frequently borrowed by marketing for controlling the development of new products. PERT, a diagramming technique for planning and evaluating progress on a project, was originally developed to control production of the Polaris atomic submarine.

A PERT chart, or network, usually has only two symbols: a circle to represent an event, and a line to represent activities between events. Events are points in time that do not consume time; activities consume time.

These steps are taken to initiate a PERT network:

1. Define the ultimate objective of the project.
2. List the principal events, or milestones, that must be reached before project completion.
3. Determine which activities must be completed to attain each milestone.
4. Determine which events are dependent upon others for completion and which can be done independently.

Events that require completion of one before the next may be started are *serial*; events that may occur concurrently are *parallel*. Events that must occur before another one can be started are *predecessor events*; events that depend on the completion of another event before they can be started are *successor events* (Fig. 14-6).

Figure 14-7 is a PERT chart for a plan to create a new product. It shows major events to be achieved in new product development. Analyze which events are serial and which are parallel. For example, the product must be defined, its demand estimated, and a preliminary budget established before the activities begin that will lead to events 4 through 9. Recall that circles represent points in time; lines represent activities. What activities do you think occur between step 11, "Begin Market Testing," and step 12, "Complete Test Analysis"?

The PERT chart in Fig. 14-7 is a simplification of the actual steps

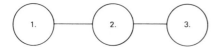

Serial events, separated by activity lines.

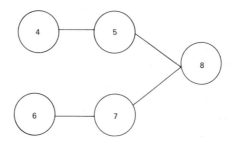

Events 4 and 5 are parallel to events 6 and 7.

Figure 14-6.   Serial and parallel events in PERT charting. Events 5 and 7 are both predecessor events to event 8.

required to develop a new product. In reality, there are hundreds or even thousands of events to be completed and coordinated in new product development.

The purpose of PERT charting is to provide management with a method of evaluating progress on and controlling complicated projects. A PERT chart sets up a plan for management to follow and graphically establishes criteria to be met as the project develops.

The key ingredient in PERT charting is estimating how long each activity will take so that target dates for each event can be established. When activity times and target dates for each event have been agreed upon, the date for project completion is established. Activity time is estimated by someone who has done the job before. A purchasing agent may estimate delivery date on raw materials; an advertising specialist knows how long it takes from selecting an advertising media to actually beginning a campaign. Statisticians have developed a method for making estimates more accurate. This method requires three estimates for each activity:

optimistic   There is only one chance in one hundred the activity can be completed in that time.
most likely   The estimator's best guess.
pessimistic   There is only one chance in one hundred that the activity will take that long.

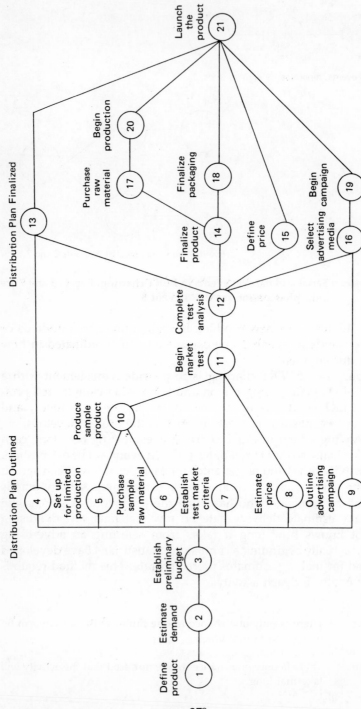

Figure 14-7. A PERT chart showing the major events to be achieved in developing a new product.

The estimates are weighted with this formula to produce the actual activity estimate.

$$\frac{1 \times \text{optimistic} + 4 \times \text{most likely} + 1 \times \text{pessimistic}}{6} = \text{activity estimate}$$

Although simple PERT charts can be constructed manually, a computer is normally required when there are more than 100 events. Software vendors provide various PERT programs that generally require only two items for input: a definition of which event precedes which other events and an estimated activity time between every pair of events. Figure 14-8 shows a PERT chart for developing a new product with estimated activity times filled in. Sample computer input based upon the data in the chart would be:

Predecessor Event	Successor Event	Activity Time
1	2	6.0
2	3	5.0
3	4	3.5
3	5	6.0
3	6	5.0
3	7	3.0
3	8	1.5
3	9	3.2

When data for each activity is coded, it is computer processed. The program first calculates the earliest that each event can be completed according to the estimates (Fig. 14-9). Notice that market testing, event 11, cannot begin until after 20.2 weeks, because of all the events that must be completed before it can be started. The chart also shows that the earliest the project can be completed is 46.2 weeks. If management decides that this is unsatisfactory, it must reexamine the estimates and determine what steps are necessary to shorten activity times.

The program further calculates the latest an event can be completed without delaying the overall project. If it is agreed that 46.2 weeks is the target date for the project, then event 13 must be completed before 43.2 weeks, event 20 before 43.2 weeks, event 18 before 45.2 weeks, and event 19 before 46 weeks. Figure 14-10 shows the earliest and latest that each event can be completed.

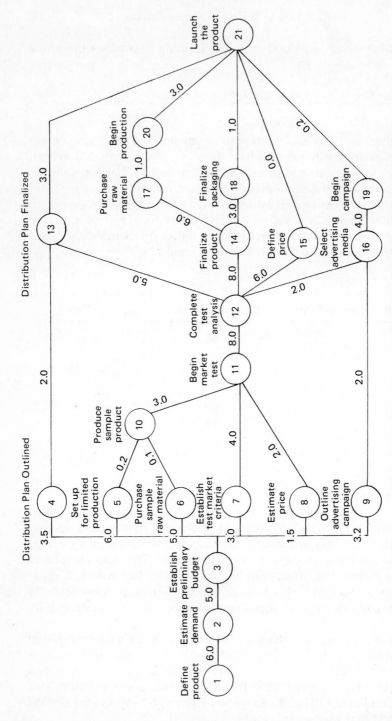

Figure 14-8.   A PERT chart for new product development with estimated activity times. All activity times are in weeks and tenths of weeks.

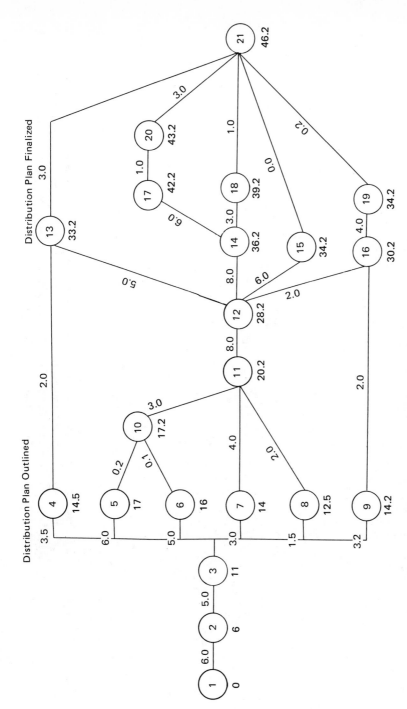

Figure 14-9. A PERT chart for new product development showing earliest date of completion for each event.

281

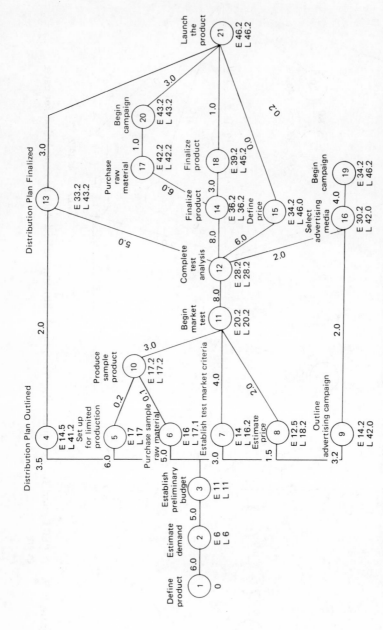

Figure 14-10. PERT chart showing early (E) and latest (L) estimates. An early estimate is the earliest time at which the event can be completed based upon the activity estimates and the estimated target dates of predecessor events. The latest estimate is the latest date by which that event can be completed without delay of the final event.

Events in which the earliest and latest dates are the same are critical events; they have no slack time, and if they are late the entire project is behind schedule. These events form the critical path (Fig. 14-11). Other events where the latest estimate exceeds the earliest estimate are on slack paths. The difference between the earliest estimate and the latest is the amount of slack time that the organization has to complete the event.

Computerized PERT charting for controlling complicated projects and new product development has these advantages:

1. Projects with hundreds or thousands of events can be organized and controlled.
2. Critical events are highlighted and priorities assigned so that they may be completed on time.
3. Budget and overtime can be properly allocated.
4. Progress can be compared with the planned schedule and remedial action taken when necessary.
5. The chart can be regularly revised, even daily, when data from actual progress is substituted for estimated activity time.
6. PERT forces managers to think through each step before a project is started.

Estimating sales, distributing products, and developing new ones are just a few of the uses that marketing organizations have found for the computer. However, in each instance, the computer is only a tool, and the ultimate factor for marketing success is intelligent decision making by an organization's management.

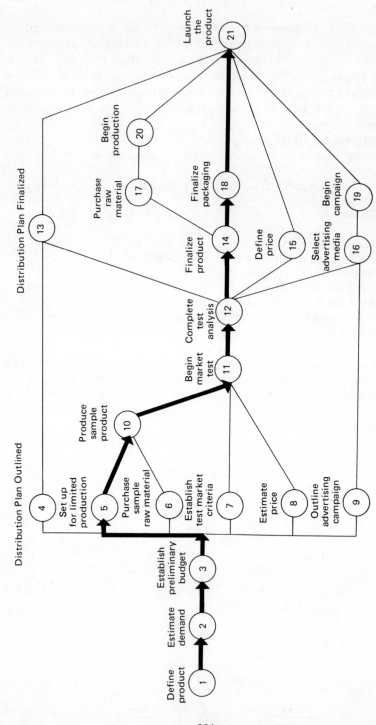

Figure 14-11. PERT chart showing path of critical events in the schedule.

MAKING IT PRACTICAL

"It's January 10th already," roared Al Westerly, executive vice-president of the Tom Terrific Toy Company. "It's time we got working on our product line for next Christmas!"

Tom Terrific Toys is a small but dynamic manufacturer of children's toys and games. Its knack for coming up with key products each year that sell well at Christmas has led to five consecutive profitable years. Mr. Westerly is the driving force behind the organization, and his instinctive decision making on marketable products is a major factor in the organization's success.

"We must have the product to the retailer by October 1, and we haven't even decided on the type of product we will be making," Westerly went on. "It's time we got that computer of ours into the marketing act!"

You have worked in Tom Terrific's data processing department for two years and are now assistant to the data processing manager. The computer, a medium-sized third generation model, successfully performs the routine accounting procedures, maintaining inventory via a daily updating, paying the bills on time, and accounting for receivables. The data processing professional staff consists of two systems analysts, five programmers with an average of three years' experience, yourself, and the data processing manager. Until now, management's only involvement with the computer system has been to review the routine reports that the computer produces and complain about the cost of installation. No marketing applications are computerized except recording sales and calculating and paying salesmen's commissions.

Prepare a two-page report for Mr. Westerly, indicating to what extent you feel the computer system can assist the marketing function this year and what steps should be taken now to prepare for future years.

REVIEW QUESTIONS

1. List four aspects of marketing.
2. What advantages does the computer give today's marketing manager?
3. List three areas in which the computer is used in marketing.
4. What advantages do marketing models have in projecting future sales?

5. List four factors that you would include in adjusting past monthly sales for forecasting future monthly sales.

6. What factors are pertinent in forecasting sales for a new product?

7. Comment on this statement: "All companies should use mathematical models in forecasting sales."

8. What is the task of the marketing manager in working with programming?

9. What steps are required to initiate a PERT network?

10. What are the advantages of using PERT in complex projects?

GLOSSARY

Activity Time—time between events in a PERT network

Critical Path—those events in a PERT network which, if behind schedule, will cause the entire project to be behind schedule

Event—point in time in a PERT chart; a milestone

Milestone—event in a PERT network that is used to measure and evaluate progress

Model—a business situation expressed in mathematical terms

PERT—Project Evaluation and Review Technique; a graphic tool for controlling and scheduling projects

Slack Path—events in a PERT network in which some slack time exists before they must be completed

15

Management Information Systems

Objectives

Many business organizations think of management information systems as a panacea to cure corporate ills. This chapter explains what management information systems are, how they are developed, and what type of information they provide management.

MANAGEMENT INFORMATION SYSTEMS

In theory, managing a business organization is simple. An organization's operation provides information about itself. Management gathers other information from outside the organization and bases its decisions on all the information available. The organization with the best information and the most talented decision makers makes the most profit.

Because of the apparent simplicity of this scheme, businessmen constantly speak of computerized decision making through management information systems. However, achieving effective decision making through computer-based systems requires managerial and technical skill found only in the most sophisticated organizations.

People often visualize the decision-making process as similar to the combat information center of a naval task force. The decision makers—senior officers in the navy, top management or the board of directors in business—scan various computerized displays of the problem at hand. A computer assimilates additional information, updates the data, and displays the current status. A small conference is held, and the chief decision maker points to a chart and says, "We'll make our main thrust here."

Computer potential makes this type of decision making possible today. Two limitations, however, reduce the computer's potential: the quality of information in the system and the ability of management to handle that information.

MANAGEMENT'S ROLE

An organization's management has these tasks to perform:

- *Planning*—the higher in the corporate structure a manager is, the further into the future he must plan
- *Decision making*—people always provide the actual decisions even in computer-based systems
- *Accepting Responsibility*—when things go wrong, it is management's fault

To plan, a manager must recognize and define corporate goals, staff to meet these goals, and organize, direct, and control the staff and the organization's information so that the goals are achieved. When these functions are done properly, the manager is in a position to make decisions for the corporate good. When the manager fails, the corporation seeks a new manager to achieve these goals more effectively.

MANAGEMENT'S ROLE IN MANAGEMENT INFORMATION SYSTEMS

Management's role in management information systems is to use the computer as an effective planning and decision-making tool. This requires management's active involvement in developing the computer-based information system so that the system provides the information required for profitable decision making.

Planning is the first responsibility of management. To plan properly, a manager must understand corporate goals. Probably the greatest shortcoming in information systems is that systems are often designed for what management thinks the corporation's goals are rather than the real objectives of the organization.

Goals must be realistic. A company with $200,000 in annual sales cannot anticipate $100,000,000 in sales over the next three years. Goals must also be quantified, that is, stated in numbers so that progress toward them can be measured. Some quantified goals are

- Market share will be 51 percent within three years.
- The clerical work force will be reduced by 10 percent by November 30.
- The Production Department will product 150,000 of these items at a unit cost of less than $1.39.
- The inventory will be reduced from an 18- to a 14-day supply.

Corporate management not only must establish goals, but also must be in position to evaluate them constantly and adjust them when necessary. Goal setting is dynamic; goals change as factors affecting the organization change. The information system must produce data for reviewing and reevaluating corporate goals.

When proper objectives are established, the corporate manager must develop the best plan to achieve these goals. The best people must be placed in key positions. These people must be given authority to develop the system so that it achieves management's goals. Performance standards must be established both for personnel and for the system. A method of measuring the system's effectiveness must be developed to see whether it is meeting the standards. The manager can then evaluate how the system is performing and take appropriate remedial action where necessary. Corporate management controls the system; the system does not control management.

In each step, management requires information on which to base its decisions. Decision making then has two primary aspects: making decisions for corporate profitability, and making decisions on the effectiveness of the information system.

Management not only must know what information it requires to make corporate decisions, but also must understand the information system sufficiently to plan, direct, and evaluate its performance.

WHY MANAGEMENT INFORMATION SYSTEMS FAIL

Almost universally, information systems fail because management fails to assume its leadership role in systems planning and development. This occurs when management:

1. Fails to understand the potential and limitations of the computer.
2. Employs outdated thinking in systems planning.
3. Becomes a spectator rather than a participant in systems development.
4. Fails to create an environment in which a management information system can be installed.
5. Does not properly see the future information needs of the organization.
6. Tries to advance too rapidly in computer systems.
7. Does not supplement the computer-based information system with sufficient information from outside the organization.
8. Does not understand the relationship of man and machine in a computer system.

Computer Potential and Limitations

With proper planning, a computer can provide services and information that lead to profit-making. A computer not only performs a company's calculations with remarkable speed, but it can select pertinent information, summarize and display it precisely, and present alternate plans of action for management's consideration. When properly programmed, it can make the routine decisions of an organization, and provide information for making more complex ones. The computer's potential is limited by the imagination and planning skills of an organization's management.

A computer can generate data so rapidly that people cannot cope with it. Management must organize and control data so that it is

- accurate—inaccurate data leads to incorrect decisions
- relevant—data must apply to the problem at hand
- concise—managers receive too much data; data must be summarized to be understandable
- timely—decisions are always made under time pressure; pertinent data must be present when a decision must be made

Outdated Thinking in Management

The computer is a reality in business today. Management must join it, not fight it. Unfortunately, the vast majority of organizations today have not mastered the technology of the computers of the mid-1960s. Most existing systems are throwbacks to the original magnetic tape and punched card versions that have merely been speeded up by the new technology. Management in these organizations has been content to survive and not grow with the computer.

Managers Are Spectators and not Participants

Developing information systems is a management function and is not to be left to the "DP people." Most data processing professionals are skilled in their field, but do not comprehend the complexities of managing a company. Corporate managers must be active in systems development from the start by defining objectives and establishing standards. This participation continues as management evaluates progress on systems development, assists in problem solving, apprises the systems technicians of changes in corporate requirements, and provides the financial and human resources needed to develop the system.

Management Fails to Create a Suitable Environment

Resistance to change is normal. Moreover, the computer constitutes a very real threat to people in an organization, in that it may either replace them or diminish their relative importance to the company. It is reasonable to expect that many people in an organization will oppose installing a computer-based information system and will slow down progress through passive resistance or indifference.

Attitude has as much to do with successful computer installation as any other factor. Computer systems cannot be thrust down people's throats. Management must create an atmosphere in which the staff realizes that a successful computer installation is good for the company and ultimately good for them. Workers must see what their roles in the developing system are, and they must be provided with the opportunity and training to grow with the new system.

Management Does Not See the Real Future Information Needs of the Organization

Management's primary task is to plan for the future. Middle managers must determine the information requirements of their departments and divisions for the coming year and subsequent years. Top managers must not only visualize company goals for perhaps ten years into the future, but must also see what information they require from the computer system to achieve these goals. Their success as managers and the success of a modern organization depend greatly on this factor.

Management Tries to Advance Too Rapidly in Computer Systems

The saying that one must crawl before he walks is appropriate in developing computer systems. A complicated tool can easily be purchased, but it is useless unless the purchaser is skilled with it.

Knowing how to use computers profitably comes only with experience. Hiring computer specialists is only a start toward a successful computer installation. Since a successful installation depends largely on its management, an organization's management must gain sufficient experience to implement a management information system. Even relatively simple data processing systems take close to a year to plan and install. A company must go through the process of installing routine computer systems and then evaluate its strengths and correct its weaknesses before contemplating the development of more sophisticated systems.

Management Does Not Supplement the Computer-based Information System

A computer-based information system never provides all the information required for corporate profitability. Information concerning competitors' activities, new techniques in data processing, business trends, and information within the organization that has not been computerized must be synthesized with computer output to complete the data for decision making.

Management Does Not Understand the Man/Machine Relationship

A computer is effective only when it interacts with people. People provide it with data, write instructions for it, and interpret its output. A computer requires managers to control it, clerks to monitor its performance, programmers to instruct it, operators to run it, and systems analysts to coordinate its performance with other corporate activities. Only when people interact effectively with the computer will the computer begin to perform adequately for an organization.

PHASES IN DEVELOPING A MANAGEMENT INFORMATION SYSTEM

Management information systems evolve over a period of years. Before reaching that level, an organization must first go through the process of automating its routine accounting functions. Accounts receivable, accounts payable, inventory, and payroll are computerized. In this phase, the computer makes some routine decisions for an organization, such as sending out dunning letters for overdue accounts and ordering replacements for inventory items whose status is below minimum level. The objectives in this phase are for an organization to familiarize itself with the problems of electronic data processing and, it is to be hoped, reduce clerical cost in the process.

When the accounting systems are installed and operating well, an organization can proceed to the next phase, which produces management reports that provide information to run a business more efficiently. The reports in this phase are basically analyses for management to study and make decisions from. These reports and some results they may effect include:

Report	Result
Salesmen's performance	realignment of sales force
Inventory status	reduction of inventory
Aged accounts receivable	improved cash flow
Rejection report for manufactured items	improved quality control
Backdated items analysis	better delivery performance
Payroll allocation	better utilization of people

During this phase, an organization begins to produce sales forecasts based upon previous sales, and to improve machine scheduling and product distribution.

Reports and anticipated results vary with each type of business, but essentially they deal with a company's key areas and attempt to pinpoint where the organization may function more effectively.

The final phase, in which the company's decision-making process is designed to center about computer-based information, requires advanced technical skill and experienced management. Two new aspects are introduced into the corporate picture: totally integrated systems designed to produce information required for decision making, and mathematical modeling for simulating business situations and analyzing alternate plans of action. When perfected, this level of sophistication will have an organization using operations research techniques depicting a company's activities in equation form to test alternate courses of action and their impact on the organization. It often takes years for this type of simulation to be effective, but when that stage is reached, companies are in a position to allocate their resources where they will provide maximum profit. However, business is constantly changing, so that even when a company can simulate its activities, the factors in the equation must be constantly changed to reflect the current status of the company (Fig. 15-1).

MEASURING THE PERFORMANCE OF MANAGEMENT INFORMATION SYSTEMS

One of management's primary responsibilities in developing management information systems is to establish standards through which systems performance is measured. Different standards are used for each phase of systems development.

In the first phase, where the organization's basic accounting procedures are automated, the customary guideline for measuring system's effectiveness has been clerical cost saving. Probably as much frustration has resulted from this as in any other area in data processing. It is rare that the initial installation of a computer saves money. Computers cost money, usually considerably more than the uninitiated anticipate. Direct computer rental or purchase price is only a small portion of the real cost of a computer installation. Greater expense is experienced in planning and developing systems, hiring qualified computer professionals, retraining the staff to work with the computer, and reeducating operating personnel and top management to

Step	Characteristics	Aim
1. Establish routine EDP procedures	Accounts payable, accounts receivable, inventory, and payroll are computerized	Establish EDP systems; reduce clerical cost
2. Use computer for more efficient organizational performance	Reduced inventories, orders filled on time, quality control improved, people used more effectively	More efficient performance in the organization
3. Use computer as a planning and decision-making tool	Simulation of product development and performance; organization's systems integrated to yield management information	Allocation of resources for maximum profit

Figure 15-1. Steps in developing a management information system.

use the computer as an effective tool. Computers are an investment in which the return is seldom immediate cash savings. Rather, the computer should accrue a series of other benefits that ultimately lead to profitibility.

The initial phase of development should be judged by these standards:

1. Possible clerical cost reduction over a period of time.
2. Improved processing, demonstrated by more accurate results produced more quickly.

In the second phase, where the computer produces reports that result in more efficient operations, the investment in the computer begins to pay off. Forecasting sales more accurately leads to efficiencies in production and inventory maintenance. Better coordinated scheduling leads to more efficient machine and man utilization. The peaks and valleys of work flow are smoothed out, overtime is reduced, and idle time is occupied. Quality control by computer leads to less waste in production and improved customer satisfaction.

Computer-related costs increase during this phase. The key to evaluating computer performance, however, is not to measure cost against cost saving, but to measure cost against cost saving plus contribution to corporate profitability. At times, the computer's benefits seem intangible, as in the relationship of improved quality control and services for customer satisfaction. For example, a bank that processes a loan application in three hours, a life insurance company that processes a death claim within 24 hours, or a wholesaler who consistently delivers his orders on time and complete, can only do this with an efficient information system. The computer's contribution to improved services and the resulting profit must be measured in analyzing the information system's effectiveness.

Another intangible, but real, factor by which the computer system's contribution to the organization may be evaluated is an improved work environment in which staff members feel more comfortable and believe that upward movement in the organization is possible. However, the bottom line, corporate profits, and the information system's contribution to it, is the ultimate standard by which the system is to be judged.

The final phase, where the computer becomes a planning and decision-making tool, is also judged ultimately by the bottom line, but more immediately by how well the system responds to the information needs of the organization. It is effective when a company's products are competitive with or better than the competitors' and when the company is consistently earning a reasonable return on its capital investments.

In this phase, an organization has the potential to do jobs that it could not do before. It can use warehouses, production and transportation facilities, and even the company's capital to maximum efficiency. But it can only do so when its management understands how to use the powerful tool that it has at its disposal.

MAKING IT PRACTICAL

You have been employed as Data Processing manager of LaFemina Fashion Shoppes for the past three years, where you have installed an IBM System/3 disk-oriented computer system virtually single-handedly. Your staff consists of one programmer-trainee and two data recorder operators.

The computer installation prepares the payroll for over 175 employees. You have also established an accounts receivable system to handle all sales on account at the store's three retail outlets. The past three years have been a struggle, but you can honestly say that the computer systems are working well.

Last week you received a memo from Linda LaFemina, the firm's president, suggesting that the organization implement a management information system during the next year. Ms. LaFamina recently attended a buyers convention and was impressed at a seminar in which the advantages of management information systems in the retail fashions business were discussed. She reasoned that since LaFemina Shoppes already had a computer operating successfully, it was well on its way to providing the type of information the decision makers at the larger department stores were receiving.

In less than two pages, prepare a memo for Ms. LaFemina in which you explain what a management information system is, what information it could possibly provide in the retail fashions business, and what you feel would be necessary to install this type of system at LaFemina Fashion Shoppes.

You be the judge in this case*

*Adapted from *Computerworld*, March 22, 1972, pp. 1–2. Copyright by *Computerworld*, Newton, Massachusetts, 02160.

Billy Mercury's automobile insurance lapsed on January 29, 1977. Two months later, on April 1, Billy was involved in a serious accident in which a pedestrian was seriously injured. The accident took place in the early morning and around noon, Billy dropped into his insurance agent's office with a check to pay a six-month premium on the policy. He informed the agent of the accident. The agent accepted the check and promptly sent it in to regional office without mentioning anything of the accident at that time. Later in the day the agent realized his mistake and notified the regional office of the accident.

The insurance company had installed a computerized system in which many of the routine decisions are handled by computer programs. The computer routinely renews policies when input transactions indicate that a check has been accepted for a policy. In the case of Billy Mercury, the policy services division received the check and computerized it in accordance with normal business practices while the claims division was investigating the accident belatedly filed by the agent. The computer, with no data concerning the accident, or the exact time that payment had been received, automatically issued a notice reinstating the policy, effective retroactively as of 12:01 A.M. on April 1, several hours before the accident occurred. A month later, the insurance company notified Mercury that the policy was not in effect until the company actually received the payment and that he was not covered for the accident. A court case followed.

The plaintiff argued that the insurance company voluntarily and intentionally waived its right not to renew the contract and that the computerized notice extended the coverage for a specific period of time. The insurance company claimed that since the renewal had been handled by its computer system to expedite service to its policyholders, it still had the right not to renew after all the facts were known.

Would you rule in favor of the plaintiff or the insurance company in this case? Can a computer system legally make decisions for an organization?

Prepare a two-page memo on your opinions in this case. Include suggestions on what the company can do to avoid similar problems in the future.

REVIEW QUESTIONS

1. What are some typical decisions frequently made by corporate management?

2. What is the role of organizational management in business?

3. What is management's role in management information systems?
4. List five reasons why management information systems fail.
5. Comment on this statement: "Top management need know only the results of a management information system. How the system arrived at these results is not its concern."
6. List several limitations of the computer's potential as a management information systems tool.
7. What qualities must data in a management information system possess?
8. Explain the relationship of the working environment to the successful implementation of a management information system.
9. Explain the three phases an organization passes through in developing a management information system.
10. How can the success of a management information system be measured?

GLOSSARY

Bottom Line—the last line on an organization's income statement, which shows either profit or loss

Goals—objectives for an organization to meet

Line Managers—people who have the responsibility of attaining the organization's goals

MIS—a management information system

Objectives—goals

Peaks and Valleys—periods of high and low activity in a business organization

Profitability—profitable performance over a period of time

Top Management—the leading members of the management team, who are directly responsible to directors for the operation of an organization

16

Planning Computer Systems

Objectives

This chapter defines for the reader the steps required to produce effective computer systems and the roles played by an organization's personnel in developing these systems.

"They took the computer out of LaFemina Fashions last week! They say that it kept making mistakes and management thought that it could do better without it."

Net income at Garfield Electrical Suppliers has increased 27 percent this past year. John Garfield, the company president, attributes this increase to tighter inventory controls resulting in better customer service. "The new, computerized inventory system is doing the job," Mr. Garfield said, "and the entire organization is benefitting from it."

Newspapers are full of stories of computer systems that fail, and yet many organizations like Garfield Electrical have successful computer operations. What did Garfield do right and where did LaFemina Fashions go wrong?

Installing a successful computer system requires extensive planning. Successful computer systems do not just happen. Months and even years of work are necessary to install an inventory system to work as effectively as Garfield's. Planning is the essential factor in developing computerized data processing systems.

Planning is essentially a management function. Good planning requires selecting proper corporate goals and developing the means of achieving these goals. Corporate management must specify what it intends to accomplish with the computer and continually direct the organization toward these goals. It must also staff the data processing and user departments with enough competent people to do the job. Most importantly, management must plan effectively if successful systems are to result.

ROLES IN SYSTEMS DEVELOPMENT

Management's Role

The primary cause for failure in computer systems is management's inability to use the computer as a business tool. Computers do not fail; an organization's management often does.

Management must take an active, ongoing role in developing computer systems. It is not sufficient to decide to install a computer and specify that payables, receivables, payroll, and inventory will be done on it. Systems goals require more precise definition and must be realistic in light of the company's financial and human resources.

Traditionally, computers have been installed to save money, but experience has taught that an organization's first computer installation is almost always more costly than anticipated. In establishing suitable goals for installing computer systems, management must consider whether the proposed system will lead to profit for the organization over a period of time. Profit can be earned by:

1. Better customer service, resulting in increased sales of the more profitable items.
2. Better management information, resulting in more profitable decision making.
3. Better and more timely information throughout the entire organization.
4. Cost savings.

Management's role in systems development continues throughout the entire process. Management must evaluate how well progress is being made and take corrective action where necessary. After allocating financial and human resources to install the system, it must continually evaluate whether its original estimates are correct. Management must also inform the systems professionals when changes in priorities occur or when circumstances, unknown to the systems people, occur that may affect the system being developed.

Data Processing Professionals

Data processing professionals have a variety of roles in installing new computer systems. They include:

- *systems design.*   The detailed plans to attain management's goals are structured by systems analysts.
- *programming.*   When the plan for installing the new system has been worked out and approved by management, programmers write the programs to perform these tasks.
- *operations.*   When the system has been designed, programmed, and tested, the data processing operations department performs all required computer tasks.

Systems Users

Systems users perform vital functions in systems development. The system is designed for them and must eventually enable them to do their jobs better. Users must be active in systems development from the initial planning stage, through detailed planning and systems design, programming, and testing so that they can use the system with maximum effectiveness.

THE SYSTEMS DEVELOPMENT CYCLE

Although the method of creating a system varies from organization to organization, these steps are common to most installations:

- Selecting appropriate systems projects
- Feasibility study
- Designing the system
- Programming
- Testing the system
- Converting to the new system
- Operating the new system

Selecting Appropriate Systems Projects

Most organizations have extensive systems needs—usually more than they can handle. The systems department, which is responsible for planning and carrying out systems changes, is usually swamped with requests to change this system, computerize that one, or see what can be done to help this department. Moreover, constant pressure exists to install new hardware and software products, particularly when they are more modern than the ones that are currently being used. Organizations have two primary limitations in selecting systems projects: money and people. Ironically, money is often not the determining factor in limiting systems undertakings. Each organization has only a limited number of truly talented systems analysts available, and these people must be assigned to the most profitable projects.

Feasibility Studies

A feasibility study is a systems project for developing the best plan for solving a company's problem. Management defines corporate systems objectives and, working with the systems department, defines priorities in undertaking systems projects. But before a proposed system is designed, a detailed plan must be put together to be sure that management's objectives will be accomplished within the time span and budget allowed. This plan is usually produced by a feasibility team composed of people from management, the systems area, and user departments.

A feasibility team examines alternate solutions to the systems problem and selects the best possible means of solving it. Ultimately, the feasibility team formulates a plan for implementing its solution in a feasibility report.

The feasibility report is the key to a successful computer installation. The more precise plan it contains, the better the chances are that the system can be designed effectively. A normal feasibility report contains:

1. A statement of the systems objectives
2. An outline of the proposed system that will achieve these objectives
3. Definitions of the files and input and output that will be required in the new system
4. An analysis of costs versus benefits in the new system
5. A plan for implementing the proposed system, including schedules for testing and conversion
6. A statement of alternate solutions available

The feasibility report is a very complete document. It is presented to management for approval or suggested changes. Without a thorough feasibility plan, systems design is greatly impeded.

Designing The System

Systems design is performed by systems analysts working with the users. Usually a system is designed by a project team, consisting of a project leader and a staff of systems analysts, programmers, and key people from the user areas.

Ordinarily, systems design is initiated by determining what output is expected from the system. This includes detailing samples of the reports that the system will provide as well as sample formats of other information that will be extracted from the system. These have been specified in general form when management defined the systems objectives, and they were clarified during the feasibility study. In the systems design phase, every anticipated output from the system is precisely defined, appropriately documented, and checked out with the users. When output is finalized, input data formats are also finalized. Programs can be designed only when all input and output formats have been specified and approved.

Systems design is time consuming, because each step must be planned with painstaking accuracy. When it is done properly, the systems designers will never hear, "This wasn't the report I expected," a month after the system is operational.

Programming

Programming can begin only after months, or, in complex systems, a year or more after the project has been initiated. Even at this point, coordination between programmers and systems analysts is vital to insure that the programs being written are solving the problems as they have been defined.

Testing

The first step in testing a system is for the programmer to test each program to be sure that it produces the specified results. When this is accomplished, programs that interact with each other (for instance, the output from one becomes the input to another) are tested together. Finally, when all programs appear to be working properly, the entire system is tested and evaluated as to whether it is ready for operation.

Two types of data for evaluating programs and systems are test data and live data. Test data is designed by the programmer to test every condition existing in the program. Test data is supplemented by live data, actual transactions from the existing system, to see whether they are handled properly.

The entire system is tested through sample transactions that are processed through the system from beginning to end. It is wise to have the system's users conduct the system's test, because they will provide a critical evaluation of the system's effectiveness, and the experience that they gain will make implementing the new system easier.

Systems Conversion

Converting from an existing system to a new one requires careful planning. Before conversion, all essential programs must be working and all data files to be used in the new system must be current. When possible, the existing system is continued for a period of time in parallel with the new one to be sure that the new system provides correct results and that no essential data has been lost in transition.

When management is satisfied that the new system's performance is acceptable, the system is turned over to the operating departments. When properly designed, the system will run for many years with only routine maintenance. Eventually, changes in the company's business requirements or in data processing hardware and software available will lead to a systems revision, and the entire systems development cycle will begin again.

MAKING THE SYSTEM WORK

An effective computer system results only after an extensive planning period. Careful thought goes into which applications to computerize or improve. A feasibility study develops a plan to implement the new system. The study produces a schedule of events, establishes budgets, and allocates the people to put in the proposed system. During the design phase, every detail of the system is planned. Effective systems usually take longer to plan and design then to program and implement.

Training all personnel involved in the system is another essential for developing effective computer systems. For users, the most effective training method is active participation in systems development from the beginning. Key user supervisors and managers should be part of the feasibility team and then should work with the system's designers on a day-to-day basis. The user staff personnel should be active in testing the new system and doing the work required for conversion.

Although management plays a key role in systems development, management training is often neglected. Managers learn computer potential and limitations best by continuing participation in the development process. Management must receive constant feedback on how the developing system is progressing, what problems are being encountered, and what new ideas have been uncovered. Corporate management is the key user of a computer system, and, as such, its role of planning, directing, and evaluating the system's performance is an active and continuing one.

Another vital aspect in developing systems is devising controls to insure the accuracy and timeliness of the system's data. Computer programs can do much of the work in verifying accuracy, but all systems require constant monitoring by people, not only to insure accuracy but to detect developing problems at their early stages and initiate remedial action.

MAKING IT PRACTICAL

American General is a 250-bed hospital located in a Boston suburb. It is contemplating installing a computer for the first time and has asked you to coordinate a training program for hospital personnel who will be involved with the computer.

American General plans to install the computer in approximately eight months and expects to have the patient billing system computerized at that time. Beyond that point the hospital's data processing plans are vague, but monitoring seriously ill patients by computer is a long-range goal.

Presently, billing is done on posting machines from source documents produced by various staff members. The computer on order has a 128K main memory and disk storage capabilities. The hospital is currently recruiting a systems analyst, two programmers, a console operator, and three data recorder operators.

The general administrator of the hospital has heard many stories of computer systems that failed because the people were not able to work with them. He is determined that this will not happen at American General.

Prepare a two-page outline of the steps that you will take in training the hospital staff. Include recommendations for training the hospital's management, professional staff, office staff, and the data processing professionals who will be designing and implementing the system.

REVIEW QUESTIONS

1. What is management's role in developing data processing systems?
2. What is the primary cause for failure in computer systems?
3. List four ways in which computer installations can lead to profit.
4. What steps compose the systems development cycle?
5. What does a feasibility report usually contain?
6. What is the role of users in systems development?
7. How are systems tested?
8. What is a parallel conversion?

9. Comment on the sentence, "Effective systems usually take longer to plan and design than to program and implement."

10. How can managers be trained to use computer systems more effectively?

GLOSSARY

Feasibility Study—a systems project for developing the best plan for solving a company's problem

Live Data—transactions from the existing system used for testing programs and the system

Profitability—profit over a period of time

Test Data—data designed by the programmer to test every condition in the program

Index